Copyright Page

Printed in the United States of America

First Printing, 2014

Library and Archives Canada Cataloguing in Publication

Zussino, Steven, 1977-, author

　　　Travel hacking for Canadians / Steven Zussino.

ISBN 978-0-9936730-0-9 (pbk.)

　　　1. Travel.　I. Title.

G151.Z88 2014　　　　　　910.2'02　　　　　C2014-900282-3

Table of Contents

About the Author

Steven Zussino is the author of Travel Hacking for Canadians. His blog, canadiantravelhacking.com shares travel hacks, tips, and deals for Canadian travelers. He decided to write this book to encourage more Canadians to travel, and to share his tips and tricks on how to make travel both fun and affordable.

Previously, he co-founded Grocery Alerts Canada with his wife Lina, where they share grocery coupons, grocery deals, and show ways for Canadians to shrink their grocery bill.

Zussino has an Honours Bachelor of Commerce degree from Lakehead University, with a major in Information Systems, as well as a Graduate Certificate in Project Management from Royal Roads University.

While on parental leave, he travelled to over four continents and thirteen countries, with his nine month old daughter.

His saving tips and advice have been featured in CNN Money, Global BC, Toronto Star, MoneySense, The Globe and Mail, and BC CTV News.

He lives in Victoria, BC with his wife and daughter.

Preface

I decided to write this book as a way to share all the travel tips and tricks I have learned. The term **travel hacking** sounds mischievous, but personally it means exploring the limits of what is possible by making your travel budget go farther through understanding how to get the best prices.

I grew up in a small city in Northern Ontario, and I always wanted to see the world and other parts of Canada. I never thought it would be realistic that I would be able to visit parts of Europe, Asia, Caribbean, Hawaii, and South America.

Using smart spending strategies and understanding the frequent flyer programs, I have been able to travel for free saving me thousands of dollars. My goal in writing this book is to make travel easier and more affordable for most Canadians. I share valuable advice in this book that can save you thousands of dollars.

I have structured this book into four sections: **Air, Accommodation, Transportation**, and **Cruising**. Throughout the book, I have included a **Tools** area at the end of each chapter to include hyperlinks to the websites mentioned in each chapter.

The first chapter in the **Air** section describes the major frequent flyer programs available to Canadians in the Canadian Frequent Flyer Programs chapter. The next chapter, **Acquiring Miles**, describes ways on how to earn frequent flyer miles in your favourite program. The **Using Miles** chapter shares my recommendations on how to use the miles or points in each program for flights. The final chapter in the Air section, **Canadian Air Travel Hacks**, shows assorted travel hacks that you can use without using any frequent flyer program.

The **Accommodation** section starts with the **Priceline / Hotwire Strategies**, where I share my personal strategies to getting to lowest prices using these websites. The **Hotel Hacks** chapter looks at ways to get the lowest price for the major travel websites and hotel chains. The **Hotel Loyalty Programs** chapter shows how each loyalty program works for individual major hotel chains. Finally, the **Alternative Hotel Options** chapter shows alternatives to staying at hotels that will stretch your travel dollars.

The **Transportation** section looks at workarounds when booking a car that can save you some money.

The **Cruising** section describes my tips and tricks to make cruising more affordable, and what to look out for.

Section 1: Air

Chapter 1

Canadian Frequent Flyer Programs

A frequent flyer program is a loyalty program offered by many airlines. Typically, airline customers enrolled in the frequent flyer program acquire miles based on the distance flown on that airline or its partners. This chapter looks at the major frequent flyer programs for Canadians, and examines the pros and cons of each program.

Aeroplan®

Aeroplan® should be a familiar program with Canadians. This is the frequent flyer program for Air Canada.

Aeroplan® Homepage.

Aeroplan® miles are earned by flying with Air Canada and other Star Alliance™ airlines. Star Alliance™ is the largest global airline network in terms of daily flights, destinations, and countries to which it flies, and number of member airlines within the alliance.

The Aeroplan® miles you earn are based on the distance you fly, and the fare option you purchase.

The Aeroplan® program rewards members who book their tickets with the highest fares. Currently, travel booked with a Tango fare (the lowest price) receives only 25% of the possible Aeroplan® Miles, and members flying in the highest fare classes, Executive Class Flexible and Executive Class Lowest, earn a 25 to 50 percent mileage bonus. When flying on partner airlines in the Star Alliance, you will generally earn 100 percent of miles flown, although mileage earning varies with the partner and fare class.

Aeroplan® has an extensive list of earning partners, including hotels, car rentals, online retailers, credit cards, financial services, and more.

When redeeming your Aeroplan® miles for travel with Air Canada, the program has two categories, ClassicFlight and Market Fare. ClassicFlight awards are capacity controlled and Market Fare awards offer access to more seats for variable mileage levels, and are only available on Air Canada and Air Canada Express.

Roundtrip economy class ClassicFlight awards within Canada and the U.S. are 15,000 miles for selected short-haul flights, and 25,000 miles for long-haul flights. Business class ClassicFlight awards are 25,000 miles for short-haul flights, and 50,000 miles for long-haul flights. Flights from Canada to Hawaii are 45,000 miles in coach, and 80,000 miles in business. Flights to Mexico, Central America, or the Caribbean are 40,000 miles in coach, and 60,000 miles in business; flights to Europe 1 are 60,000 miles in coach, and 90,000 miles in business; and to flights to Asia 1 are 75,000 miles in coach and 150,000 miles in business.

Market Fare Flight Rewards offer access to a greater choice of flight departures, routes, and travel times at higher mileage levels on Air Canada flights.

If you travel enough with Air Canada and their select airline partners, you can qualify for elite status. As an Elite, Super Elite, or Prestige member, you can enjoy great benefits, upgrades, and even bonus Aeroplan® miles on every flight.

Aeroplan has created another program called Distinction. The program awards the top accumulating Aeroplan® members with Distinction status and benefits. The great thing about Distinction is that you can earn Distinction miles without even flying!

Eligible miles are miles earned in the Aeroplan® Program directly at participating partners and include base and certain bonus mile offers. Unless otherwise indicated at the time of offer, the following miles are not eligible for Distinction status: financial card sign-up; bonus miles received as a benefit of the Air Canada Altitude program or Aeroplan® Distinction status; miles accumulated through conversion from other programs or transfers between member accounts, top-up miles, contest prizes, and reinstated miles.

Here is a breakdown of the different Distinction levels:

Level	How to Qualify
dSilver	*25,000 eligible miles accumulated during the calendar year.*
dBlack	*50,000 eligible miles accumulated during the calendar year.*
dDiamond	*100,000 eligible miles accumulated during the calendar year.*

For any given calendar year, Distinction status is based on the number of eligible miles earned by a member between January 1 and December 31 of the previous calendar year. For example, 2015 Distinction status is based on the number of eligible miles earned by a member in 2014. Members who reach a certain level during the qualifying year will be eligible to receive the benefits immediately upon achieving a certain level and their new Distinction status will be valid until December 31 of the following calendar year.

Members are required to requalify for Distinction status for the following year. For example, those members who enjoyed Distinction status in 2015 must earn the required number of eligible miles in 2015 to continue to enjoy Distinction status in 2016.

Here are some of the benefits having Distinction in the Aeroplan program:

1. Reduced mileage levels on Market Fare Flight Rewards. **Distinction members get up to 35% off.**

2. Distinction Flights.
   Distinction members receive an invitation for flights leaving from major Canadian cities for peak period travel to popular destinations. 100% of the seats are reserved exclusively for Distinction members and offered at the ClassicFlight Rewards mileage level.

3. Air Canada Getaway Bonus on eligible roundtrips.
   Get up to 1,500 Distinction bonus miles for every eligible roundtrip that includes a Saturday night stay when you fly with Air Canada to more than 25 popular destinations such as Florida, New York, California, London and Paris.

4. Distinction bonus on hotel stays accumulation.
   dDiamond and dBlack members get 250 Distinction bonus miles per stay with Fairmont Hotels & Resorts, Marriott® and Starwood Hotels & Resorts®, on up to 20 stays per year, for up to a maximum of 5,000 Distinction bonus miles per calendar year. This is in addition to the base miles they will earn per stay. To be eligible for this bonus, members must earn miles in the Aeroplan® Program at the time of stay. Fairmont redemption stays are also eligible for this bonus.

5. Bonus with Aeroplan eStore.
   Get up to 3X the miles per dollar spent when you shop online with your favourite Aeroplan® eStore retailers.

On the Aeroplan® website, you will see all the options they have available, including flights, hotels, car rentals, activities, merchandise, and vacation packages. These additional options are great for added flexibility, but redeeming for flight rewards usually gives you the best return for your Aeroplan® miles.

Positives:

- Large number of Canadian retailers available to earn Aeroplan® miles (From Sobeys to Esso).

- Excellent value for short-haul flights (i.e. Toronto to New York, Vancouver to Edmonton), with just 15,000 Aeroplan® miles required.

- Air Canada allows for a free stopover on any ClassicFlight reward ticket redemption (i.e. so you can stop in Toronto for your flight from Vancouver to St. Johns).

- You can earn and redeem Aeroplan® miles for flights on regional Canadian carriers (non-Star Alliance™ members): Bearskin Airlines (Manitoba and Northern Ontario), Air North (flyairnorth.com), and the Yukon Territories' official airlines, which reach eight destinations in the Yukon, Northwest Territories, British Columbia, Alberta and Alaska, as well as Canadian North (canadiannorth.com) and First Air (firstair.ca). Central Canada is served by Calm Air (calmair.com), which features destinations in Manitoba and Nunavut; and Bearskin Airlines (bearskinairlines.com), which serves Ontario, Manitoba and Quebec.

Negatives:

- Aeroplan® imposes hefty fuel surcharges when booking with many Star Alliance partners, including Air Canada.

- Challenges of earning many Aeroplan® miles when booking low cost Tango fares.

- Charges for award changes and cancellations with award travel bookings.

- Lack of availability of flights for Classic Flight rewards.

- 12-month mileage expiration policy. In order to keep your Aeroplan® account active and to avoid the expiration of all miles in the account, you must make at least one qualifying transaction every 12 months.

AIR MILES®

This is another popular loyalty program in Canada, boasting over 10 million active members, representing approximately two-thirds of all Canadian households.

The AIR MILES® program is different from the other programs, because the miles are earned not by flying but by spending money at Canadian retailers. AIR MILES® has more than 260 retail and online partner sponsors, including Bank of Montreal™, American Express™, Shell Canada™, Canada Safeway™ in Western Canada, Metro™ and Rexall/PharmaPlus™ pharmacies in Ontario, and Sobeys™ and Lawton Drugs™ in the Atlantic provinces east of Ontario.

They also have a Gold program where they provide members with exclusive benefits including flight and merchandise discounts, and Gold-only Sponsor Bonus Offers. You can become a Gold member when you earn 1,000 miles in one year and by shopping at five different AIR MILES sponsors.

The AIR MILES® website has a chart for each province that shows how many miles you need to travel to your destination.

Positives:

- Large number of Canadian retailers available to earn miles.
- 11 airline partners, including Air Canada and WestJet, to redeem miles for travel to over 500 destinations worldwide.
- No blackout periods.
- You can earn AIR MILES® at over 140 online Canadian and U.S. stores.
- Good value for expensive short flights within province (i.e. Thunder Bay to Toronto, Victoria to Prince George).
- Occasional flight specials that reduce the AIR MILES® required by up to 40%.
- Easy reward redemption chart displaying fixed number reward miles for a flight.

Negatives:

- No way to earn miles flying, unless booking through Sponsor travel agency Marlin Travel, Transat Holidays, or Travelocity.ca
- Extra costs for flight redemption. You must pay applicable taxes, fees and surcharges, excess baggage costs, transportation and government fees, and other non-ticket costs.

- No cancellations or refunds are permitted once a travel reward is booked.

- Cannot redeem for business or first class tickets unless you hold the American Express® AIR MILES® Reserve Credit Card.

- Reservations must be made at least two days in advance.

Alaska Airlines®

This is a great frequent flyer program for Canadians living in Alberta and British Columbia. This airline flies from Victoria, Vancouver, Kelowna, Calgary, and Edmonton in Canada to cities in Alaska, Hawaii, the lower 48 states, and Mexico.

Alaska Airlines® does not belong to any global airline alliance like the Star Alliance™, but you do have the opportunity to earn and redeem miles across airlines from different alliances. This program makes sense for flyers that do not fly frequently enough in the United States with either Delta or American to achieve any type of Elite status with those carriers. You can credit the miles that you would earn flying those airlines to your Alaska Airlines® mileage account, making this a flexible program.

Members of this program earn one mile per mile flown on Alaska Airlines® and their partners. You earn a minimum of 500 miles for short hops, i.e. Victoria, British Columbia to Seattle, Washington. First class fares earn 50 percent additional bonus miles, and Full Flex fares earn an additional 25 percent. Earning varies with partner airlines, and most offer actual flight miles with fewer miles for discounted coach fares and more miles for higher fare classes.

Alaska Airlines® has many bonus mile offers on its website. They reward travel booked through Alaska Airlines® Vacations and premium fares booked (First, Business and Premium economy class tickets) with their airline partners.

They also have one of the top travel reward credit cards available for Canadians, the Alaska Airlines® Platinum MasterCard Credit Card.

This card features:

- 25,000 Bonus Miles upon approval.

- An annual coach Companion Fare from $110 (USD) ($99 base fare plus taxes and fees, from $11 depending on your Alaska Airlines® flight itinerary).

- One mile for every $1 spent on qualifying net retail purchases.

- Three miles for every dollar in qualifying net retail purchases of Alaska Airlines® flights and vacation packages.

I have this credit card, and I really enjoy having the companion fare certificate. I use this for long-haul flights in North America to Florida or Hawaii, where the fares can be high flying from British Columbia.

You have the option of using one-way or round-trip awards at three levels of redemption: Super Saver, Choice, and Full Flex for flights with Alaska Airlines. You can also redeem miles with fifteen other carriers, including American Airlines, British Airways, Delta, Emirates, and KLM.

If you travel enough with Alaska Airlines® and their select airline partners, you can qualify for elite status. As an MVP, MVP Gold, or Gold 75K member, you can enjoy great benefits, special treatment, and even bonus miles on every flight.

I have redeemed my Alaska Airlines® miles for flights on the floatplane from Victoria to Seattle's Lake Union with former partner Kenmore Air, flights to Miami, San Diego, Los Angeles, and for a trip to London, England with partner American Airlines.

Positives:

- Alaska allows one stopover of more than 24 hours or one open jaw on international awards.

- As long as you keep your account active, by earning or spending at least one mile every 24 months, your miles will never expire.

- Option of using Money & Miles for a discount off of a purchased ticket.

- Can earn Elite status by flying with other partner airlines.

Negatives:

- Not too many retail partners in the program for Canadians, so you need to get an affiliated credit card or fly frequently to earn mileage.
- Not a member of any major airline alliance.

British Airways Avios

Avios is the loyalty program for British Airways. This airline flies from Vancouver, Calgary, Edmonton, Toronto, Montreal to cities in Europe. Additionally, they have a code-share with WestJet that lets you earn Avios.

One major benefit of the Avios program is that you can combine Avios points from different Avios schemes (British Airways and Iberia Airlines) into one family member's accounts. This can make it easier to redeem your acquired points.

The Avios program works on distance, so you can find some great buys. A one-way flight between Toronto and New York can be had for only 4,500 Avios points (9,000 round trip), compared to 15,000 Aeroplan Miles for the same flight (round-trip).

Positives:

- No blackout dates for redemption.
- Can create a Household Account that enables you to share your Avios with the other members of your household for free.
- Fantastic redemptions with Avios on short-haul flights (Montreal or Toronto to New York) using American Airlines (9,000 round trip).

Negatives:

- No retail partners in Canada to earn extra Avios.
- Charged for extra stopovers as an additional flight.
- Major fuel surcharges charges.

Starwood Preferred Guest®

Starwood Preferred Guest® (SPG) is the loyalty program for the Starwood hotels chain (Westin, Sheraton, Four Points by Sheraton, W Hotels, Le Meridien, St. Regis, The Luxury Collection, Aloft, and Element).

©2014 Starwood Hotels & Resorts Worldwide, Inc. All Rights Reserved. SPG, Preferred Guest and their logos are the trademarks of Starwood Hotels & Resorts Worldwide, Inc. or its affiliates and are being used with the express permission of Starwood Hotels & Resorts Worldwide, Inc.

You mainly earn miles on stays at Starwood properties, but this program has partnerships with over thirty airlines including Aeroplan, Air France/KLM, Alaska, American, ANA, British Airways, Delta, Emirates, Lufthansa, Singapore, US Airways, United, and Virgin Atlantic.

This is a highly desirable program because of its points-to-miles transfers offering a 5,000-mile bonus when you transfer 20,000 points. For example, if I transfer 20,000 SPG points to Aeroplan, I would have 25,000 Aeroplan miles. I have seen transfer bonuses in the past year with Avios where you could earn a 25% bonus on the miles transferred to Avios, earning 31,250 Avios when transferring SPG points.

SPG points do not expire as long as you earn, redeem, or purchase points at least once every 12 months. Points can be transferred for no cost between accounts only by members of the same household. Standard room award nights have no blackout dates or capacity controls.

If you are a SPG Platinum or Gold member, you also earn one Starpoint® for every dollar spent on eligible Delta flights. Additionally, SPG Platinum members enjoy Elite benefits when traveling with Delta, such as priority check-in, Priority Boarding, and first checked bag free.

Benefits:

- Major bonuses for transferring SPG points to airlines frequent flyer programs.
- Many redemption options without transfer.

Negatives:
- No retail partners to earn many SPG points.
- If not a frequent traveler, you must have an affiliated credit card to really earn enough points.

VIPorter

VIPorter is the loyalty program for Porter Airlines. This airline flies from Halifax, Moncton, Montréal, Mont-Tremblant, Ottawa, Québec City, Sault Ste. Marie ON, St. John's, NL, Sudbury, Thunder Bay, Timmins, Toronto, and Windsor to U.S. cities like Boston, Chicago, Washington, D.C., and New York.

You earn 375 VIPorter Points with a Firm Class ticket (one-way flight), 750 points for a Flexible Class ticket (one-way flight), and 1,500 points for a Freedom Class ticket (one-way flight). To redeem your VIPorter Points, you need 7,500 points for a one-way flight. All points expire after four years from their earning date. VIPorter Points can only be used to pay for the cost of the fare. Passengers booking with points are responsible for all applicable taxes and fees. Approximately 10% of Porter's available seats are allocated for VIPorter redemption. Availability is not guaranteed on all Porter flights.

Positives:
- No blackout dates for redemption.
- Simple redemption plan.

Negatives:
- Can't earn points flying with partners.
- No ability to buy points (to top up).
- No credit card to earn extra points.

WestJet Dollars

Westjet has recently established its loyalty program. You earn WestJet dollars on flights operated by WestJet and American Airlines, using the affiliated WestJet RBC MasterCard credit card, and with car rentals and hotel bookings from their website.

WestJet dollars can be used like cash towards the purchase of WestJet flights and WestJet Vacations packages. You can use your WestJet dollars on any date, to any WestJet destination, with no blackout periods. A minimum balance of $25 in WestJet Reward dollars is required for redemption.

Here is a breakdown on how you can earn WestJet dollars:

Spending Requirement	Return
Spend between $1 and $1,499 annually on WestJet flights	*Earn 1% back in WestJet dollars or 0.5% back on WestJet Vacation packages*
Spent $1,500 on WestJet flights in your qualifying year	*Earn a bonus of $35 WestJet dollars, and start earning 2.5% back in WestJet dollars or 1% back on WestJet Vacations packages.*
Spend $4,500 annually	*Earn a companion flight anywhere WestJet flies in Canada – you can purchase one round-trip flight and only have to pay the taxes, fees, and surcharges for the second person on the same itinerary. You will also get two lounge passes and four advance seat selection vouchers.*
Spend $6,000 annually	*You earn another companion ticket, this time to anywhere WestJet flies, including Canada, the U.S., Mexico, the Caribbean, and Central America. This means you can purchase one round-trip flight, and only have to pay the taxes, fees, and surcharges for the second person on the same itinerary. You will also get another chance to choose the seats you want with four advance seat selection vouchers, and the ability to relax with two airport lounge passes.*

WestJet Rewards uses a 12-month period, starting from the date you enroll in the program, for when they track your annual spending.

Positives:

- No blackout dates for redemption.
- Do not need to have a lot of points to redeem and earn a reward versus most frequent flyer programs.

Negatives:

- Not too many retail partners. To acquire WestJet dollars, you need to get their affiliated credit card or fly frequently.
- Not a member of any airline alliance.
- Low earnings for WestJet bookings (flights, car rentals, and hotels).
- WestJet Vacations spending, partner marketed flights, partner bookings made on westjet.com, taxes, fees, surcharges, and insurance don't count towards your annual qualifying spending.

Tools

- Aeroplan - http://www.aeroplan.com
- Air Miles - http://www.airmiles.ca
- Alaska Airlines – http://www.alaskaairlines.com
- Avios – http://www.ba.com
- Starwood Preferred Guest – http://www.starwood.com
- Porter Airlines – http://www.flyporter.com
- WestJet – http://www.westjet.ca

Chapter 2

Acquiring Miles

One of the best ways to rack up frequent flyer miles is usually being a frequent flyer. However, getting into an airplane is not the only way to earn frequent flyer miles. Since I no longer travel for work, I have to find new ways to acquire frequent flyer miles. This chapter shares many ways to earn frequent flyer miles without flying.

Reclaim Recent Flights

Most airlines let you claim miles months after you have flown. Double-check your last flights, and verify that you received mileage credit. Each program has different requirements for the mileage credit request (could be up to 12 months from the travel date).

You'll just need your ticket, seat, and flight number. Generally you can find these in your email confirmations, and if you can't find the seat number, a call to the airline usually does the trick.

Online Shopping

Did you know that most major frequent flyer programs have an online shopping portal? Air Miles, Aeroplan, RBC Rewards, American Airlines, and Avios all have malls where you can earn miles for every dollar you spend. They have popular retailers like Sears®, Chapters, Dell, eBay®, The Gap®, and The Bay.

You need to sign in the shopping portal first before making your purchase on the retailer's website. You can sometimes earn large bonuses at certain retailers of up to ten bonus miles per dollar (at the Gap® recently).

Here is an example of a promotion where you would earn up to 10 x the regular Aeroplan® miles per $1 spent.

5X TO 10X THE MILES AND NO LINEUPS
From November 29, 2013, to December 3, 2013

There's no better way to kick off your holiday shopping than with a spectacular Black Friday/Cyber Monday offer. Earn 5X to 10X the miles through eStore!

DETAILS   TERMS & CONDITIONS

For five days only, take advantage of a supersized offer throughout the Black Friday and Cyber Monday shopping weekend through Aeroplan eStore. Enjoy 5X to 10X the miles from the comfort of your own home!

From November 29 to December 3, 2013 only, enjoy all the perks of Black Friday/Cyber Monday shopping madness without having to stand in endless lineups or battle crowds. Get all your holiday shopping done online through Aeroplan Store and earn 5X to 10X the miles. Get gifts for them and miles for you!

Aeroplan eStore has an incredible range of over 100 retailers to shop from. From stylish clothing to the latest in electronics, you'll find many of the most popular brands:

- Dell
- Apple Store Canada
- Hudson's Bay
- Indigo.ca
- ebay.ca
- Gap
- And many more!

To earn 5X to 10X the Aeroplan Miles, simply go to the Aeroplan eStore website, log in with your Aeroplan Number, and start shopping. Your miles will be automatically added to your account with every transaction.

Enjoying a mega offer on holiday shopping from home. Just another advantage of being a member.

This special Black Friday/Cyber Monday offer is on for five days only. Hurry to take advantage - offer ends December 3rd.

Sample Aeroplan® Promotion.

What I like about this shopping method is that you can also use any coupon codes that you may find elsewhere and still earn miles. It's amazing - they take you to the exact website, but as long as you click through the mileage mall, you get miles. These can really add up quickly!

This can be a great way to earn bonus miles, especially for big purchases. Most of the time, as long as you are logged into your account and clicked through to the retailer from the mall, you won't have any problem seeing the bonus miles post up.

I always recommend taking a screenshot of the purchase and the clickthrough, in case the miles do not appear in your account.

My final tip is to purchase a gift card through the mall to double-dip your bonus miles.

Here is what you do:

1. Buy a gift card at the mall to receive the initial frequent flyer miles.

2. When you receive the gift card (electronically or through the mail, purchase the products with the gift card through the mall again to double-dip your bonus miles!

Subscriptions and Services

Another great way to boost your frequent flyer miles is taking a closer look at your monthly subscriptions. Some magazine subscriptions (like Chatelaine, MoneySense, Canadian Business), phone plans (Primus), and chequing accounts (BMO and CIBC), all can earn you frequent flyer miles.

Give your opinion

Many survey websites award frequent flyer miles or points for your opinions. Once you register and fill out a profile or questionnaire, you will be invited to fill out surveys to earn extra miles. These websites do not cost you anything other than your time. Remember that these miles will not add up quickly. Most frequent flyer programs require you to earn or redeem miles at least once every 12-18 months. If you don't, you might forfeit any miles you have in the account. Making small deposits through these survey sites will help you keep any dormant accounts active.

Here is a breakdown of some of the survey reward websites for Canadians:

1. e-Rewards

Joining e-Rewards is free, and by invitation only by their frequent flyer partners. These partners include: Air Miles, Alaska Airlines®, American Airlines, Choice Privileges, Hertz®, Hilton® Honors™, IberiaPlus, Priority Club, United, and US Airways. Once you sign up with a frequent flyer program, they will send you an invitation to join e-Rewards. Make sure that you enable e-mail updates so the frequent flyer program can contact you with an invitation.

2. Asking Canadians

Asking Canadians is an online community that rewards you for sharing your opinions. For every online survey that you participate in, you'll automatically earn your choice of HBC Rewards points, Aeroplan® Miles, or Petro-Points.

The e-mail invitations that I have received range from awarding 75 Aeroplan® miles for a 20 minute length survey. I usually find that the estimate for the length of the survey is not very accurate, but understand that the amount of Aeroplan® miles awarded will range from 25 to 100.

Here is an example of an email invitation Asking Canadians sent.

Asking Canadians survey.

Real Estate

You can earn frequent flyer miles with AIR MILES® and Aeroplan® with various real estate companies.

AIR MILES®

Century 21 is the only company in the Canadian real estate industry to offer AIR MILES® rewards for the purchase or sale of a home. You will receive two AIR MILES® for every $1,000 bought or sold through a participating Century 21 office to a maximum of 1,500 reward miles per transaction. When selling a property, your home must be listed with a Century 21 office to be eligible to earn reward miles.

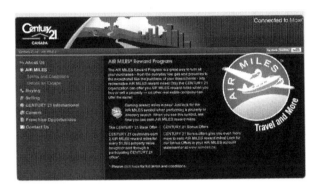

Century 21 – Canadian AIR MILES® sponsor.

As an example, if you sold your home at $400,000 and listed with Century 21, you would receive 800 AIR MILES®.

Aeroplan

Aeromove is a home and moving services program available exclusively to Aeroplan® Members. Aeromove has partnered with real estate agents from multiple real estate companies across Canada. Participating brokerages include: Royal LePage, Re/Max, Coldwell Banker, Prudential, and Sutton Group.

Aeromove homepage.

You will receive 1,500 Aeroplan® Miles for every $10,000 of your house price that you buy and/or sell.

This table below shows the summary of the potential Aeroplan® miles that you can earn on a transaction with Aeromove:

Home Value	Potential Aeroplan Miles
$200,000	30,000
$300,000	45,000
$500,000	75,000
$750,000	112,500
$1,000,000	150,000

Here is how the process works with Aeromove in order to collect Aeroplan® miles from a real estate transaction. From the Aeromove website, you click on the Request an Agent hyperlink from the Buying area. You need to fill out an online request form to request a real estate agent to work with.

Within two business days, your assigned Real Estate Agent will contact you. You then have the option to work with that agent provided, or ask Aeromove to request a different agent. Once your real estate transaction has completed using the referred real estate agent, the Aeroplan® Miles will be credited to your Aeroplan® account.

Some of the other real estate transactions that can earn you miles include:

- 500 Aeroplan® Miles for full service moves from Atlas Van Lines for less than 150 miles, and 2,500 Aeroplan® Miles for moves over 150 miles.

- 500 Aeroplan® Miles for every home inspection service from Amerispec.

- 500 Aeroplan® Miles for each staging consultation and two Aeroplan® Miles per $1 spent on staging services.

- One Aeroplan® Mile for every $1 you spend on junk removal services from 1-800-GOT-JUNK.

- One Aeroplan® Mile for every $1 you spend on legal services from Danson Schwarz Recht.

Buying miles

Most travelers don't think about it, but frequent flyer miles have a real cash value. The problem is the cash value is different for every traveler. If you can figure out how much a mile is worth to you, you can find some good values.

For example, if you enjoy flying in business class, you may find that spending up to $0.04 cents a mile can be a good deal because of the value you get from those miles. If a desired business class flight costs over $5,000 and you can spend over $2,000 on miles or points to redeem a free flight you are saving over 60% of the regular price.

All of the major airlines and frequent flyer programs allow you to buy a certain amount of miles every year. Sometimes each program or airline has promotions where you can earn bonuses up to 100%.

Here is my process on how I evaluate whether or not to purchase frequent flyer miles:

1. Determine a rough value per mile. A flight from Victoria, British Columbia to Thunder Bay, Ontario would cost 25,000 Aeroplan miles. A ticket can cost nearly $700 with taxes, so dividing the cost of the ticket and the miles required to fly, I get a return of 2.8 cents. This is my personal valuation for each frequent flyer mile in this particular program using a domestic flight.

2. Look for discount promotions where you pay less than your value per mile. I would strongly look closely at any promotion from a Star Alliance airline or Aeroplan selling miles at a price lower than 2.8 cents per mile. Personally, redeeming Aeroplan miles is more challenging than simply buying a ticket, due to limits on availability, so the discount must be worth it.

Buying miles is not the cheapest way to acquire frequent flyer miles, but I believe it is the easiest method.

Groceries

Some grocery store chains across Canada offer frequent flyer miles with a purchase. Some of these chains include: Safeway, Metro, Sobeys, and Thrifty Foods. I personally find that the regular prices at these stores are higher to pay for the cost of giving frequent flyer miles. However, if you time your purchases combining with their bonus mile promotions, you could easily earn hundreds of extra miles.

Safeway

Safeway is a grocery chain in Western Canada (British Columbia, Alberta, Saskatchewan, Manitoba, and Northern Ontario). You earn one AIR MILE® for every $20 spent in grocery purchases within a single transaction after all discounts and exclusions are applied.

This store has many coupons and promotions available to earn bonus AIR MILES®. I took part in a recent promotion where I purchased five boxes of All Bran cereal for $4.99 each. Purchasing five boxes earned a bonus 100 AIR MILES®. I used a $2 off coupon on each box of cereal to bring down the total out of pocket expense to just $14.95. You are able to use coupons with any AIR MILES® promotions to reduce your cost per mile.

I also recommend shopping at Safeway on Customer Appreciation Day, the first Tuesday of each month. If you have a purchase greater than $35 you have the option to earn 10 times the base reward miles.

If you are buying any AIR MILES® specials and they no longer have any quantity, you should request a rain check. When you get your rain check, ask for multiples of the rain check so that instead of buying just five to get 50 AIR MILES®, if you bought 50 you would get 500 Air miles.

If you time your purchases combining with their bonus mile promotions, you could easily earn hundreds of extra AIR MILES®.

Metro

Shopping at the Metro grocery store chain in Ontario and Quebec you can earn one AIR MILES® reward mile for every $20 spent. By picking up designated bonus AIR MILES® items throughout the store you will have the opportunity to earn extra AIR MILES®.

Sobeys

Sobeys grocery stores are located across Canada. You are able to earn base points of one Club Sobeys point for every whole dollar spent, or you can earn bonus points on selected products in participating Sobeys stores. Club Sobeys points are transferrable to Aeroplan at a ratio of two to one, so transferring 100 Club Sobeys points to Aeroplan would earn you 50 Aeroplan® miles.

Thrifty Foods

Thrifty Foods is a grocery chain based on Vancouver Island and the lower Mainland in British Columbia. Club Thrifty Foods is a Points rewards program that has no cost to join. You receive one Club Thrifty Foods Point for every whole dollar spent, and you can earn Bonus Points on selected products at all Thrifty Foods stores.

Once you have earned enough Club Thrifty Foods Points, you can opt to have your Points auto-converted to Aeroplan® Miles.

Register for their emails, as this program will send many exclusive printable and electronic coupons that you can load on your card.

Book your hotel rooms with RocketMiles

Rocketmiles is a travel booking site that helps travellers earn 7,000 airline miles per booking, or about 10-20 times the typical incentive. You can currently earn miles from Aeroplan®, Alaska Airlines Mileage Plan, American Airlines AAdvantage, Etihad Guest, Flying Blue, Frontier EarlyReturns, HawaiianMiles, JetBlue TrueBlue, United MileagePlus, US Airways Dividend Miles, and Virgin America Elevate.

Rocketmiles

Rocketmiles was created to offer travelers a lucrative new option that allows them to earn miles even faster and when booking hotels. Rocketmiles customers can book rooms at desirable premium hotels for similar rates as found on popular online travel agencies and at the same time earn frequent flyer reward miles.

Rocketmiles has launched a partnership with Aeroplan®, enabling Aeroplan® members to earn thousands of Aeroplan miles on hotel bookings in Canada and throughout the world.

Aeroplan® members can earn up to 5,000 Aeroplan® miles for each hotel night booked. Rocketmiles features premium hand-picked hotels in hotspots around the globe.

Before booking a room with Rocketmiles, you should understand the positives and negatives of using their website.

Positives:

- Rocketmiles delivers a hand-picked selection of premium hotels that appeal to business travelers, as opposed to the hundreds of search results which aggregators offer, while also offering the same prices.

- When I made several reservations, the Rocketmiles rate was similar to the hotel website's rate and I earned thousands of bonus Aeroplan and Alaska Airlines miles.

Negatives:

- Rocketmiles is unable to guarantee that the reservation will count toward elite status with your hotel's loyalty program. Each hotel loyalty program does not make the same guarantee, and has advised that situations are treated on a case-by-case basis, with the ultimate decision being made by the specific property's reservation management staff.

- The inventory in smaller cities is quiet limited, but I was able to find many hotels in most popular Canadian and U.S. cities.

Transfer from other programs

Did you know that you can transfer points from less frequently used programs to Aeroplan® and AIR MILES®?

Here is a brief summary of loyalty programs and the frequent flyer programs where you can transfer to:

AIR MILES®

You can transfer from HBC Rewards to AIR MILES®.

Aeroplan

This program has several partners that let you gain Aeroplan miles a lot faster.

- Club Sobeys
- Esso Extra (through Club Sobeys)
- Starwood Preferred Guest®
- American Express Rewards
- Hertz Gold Plus Rewards® Points
- Hilton HHonors
- Club Carlson
- Best Western Rewards

- American Express Membership Rewards

Starwood Preferred Guest®

You can transfer to several popular airline frequent flyer programs including: Aeroplan®, American Airlines, United Airlines, US Airways, and British Airways Avios.

The Starwood® points can be converted at a 1:1 rate, with a 5,000 mile bonus for every 20,000 miles you transfer.

Travel Related Services

Most travel related services can also earn you frequent flyer miles. Everything from car rentals, hotel stays, and cruises can earn you frequent flyer miles. One tip I have is that if you find you want to redeem your miles for flights, to make sure that your hotel rewards are forwarded to the frequent flyer program of your choice.

Always ask for mileage credit with a stay, and have your mileage account number handy. Even small amounts of miles add up eventually, so don't let an opportunity to earn points pass you by.

As you can see, there are lots of ways to boost the miles in your account balance. However, one of the top mileage boosters is a credit card application.

Credit Card Applications (getting miles without flying)

Signing up for credit cards to earn frequent flyer miles is the easiest and quickest way to earn miles and points for free travel. You can sometimes earn as many as 50,000 miles for a single card.

Now before you start applying for credit cards, you need to take a closer look at a few things:

Check your credit history

Your credit history is recorded in files maintained by at least one of Canada's major credit-reporting agencies: Equifax Canada and TransUnion Canada. It is possible to obtain your credit file for free. Please consult the agencies' websites in order to obtain more information. These files are called credit reports. A credit report is a snapshot of your credit history. It is one of the tools lenders use to determine whether or not to give you credit.

To get your all-important credit score, you'll have to spend some money. Both Equifax Canada and TransUnion Canada offer consumers real-time online access to their credit score (your credit report is also included).

Before you actually apply for a new credit card, I would recommend getting your free annual credit report, and making sure that all of your accounts are in good standing. You will want to make sure that you have no credit card debt, that you have a high credit score, and that you can pay your credit card balance in full each month.

Minimum spending requirements

Many credit cards require you to complete a certain amount of minimum spending before you get the sign-on bonus (i.e. spending $1,000 in the first three months of having the credit card). While $1,000 in three months may sound like a lot, that comes out to under $350 a month for three months.

To satisfy these minimum spending requirements, make sure that you put all of your finances on your credit cards. Use cash only when you absolutely have to!

If you charge your groceries, gasoline, cable, cell phone, vacation, shopping, dining out on your credit card, it is fairly easily to meet the minimum spending requirements in the designated time period.

Annual Fee

Another important factor to consider when looking at a credit card is the annual fee.

Many of the credit cards will have an annual fee attached to them. Some of the cards will have annual fees that can be as high at $699. The credit cards with the higher annual fees have more benefits, including higher mileage benefits.

The annual fee will sometimes be waived for the first year. If you enjoy the benefits of the credit card, and do not want to cancel the credit card, consider requesting that the credit card company waive the annual fee.

When an annual fee comes due on a card, you can often get the bank to waive it by downgrading to a related card with no adverse credit effect, or by speaking to the retention department to receive some bonus (statement credit or annual fee waived).

Having powerful cards with big sign-up bonuses is the easiest way to jumpstart your collection of frequent flyer miles.

Below are my recommendations for the top overall cards:

American Express Gold Rewards Card

This is a travel credit card that offers flexible rewards. You are able to transfer your points to frequent flyer programs like, Aeroplan®, Alitalia, British Airways Avios, Cathay Pacific Asia Miles, Hilton HHonors, and Starwood, or you can charge any travel to the card then pay for it with points that you receive with your spending.

American Express Gold Rewards Card.

You earn two points for every $1 in Card purchases at eligible gas stations, grocery stores and drugstores in Canada and eligible travel purchases, including flights, hotels, car rentals, cruises, and more. You earn one point for every $1 in Card purchases everywhere else.

You have the option to transfer each point on a 1:1 basis to Aeroplan® and other programs (other programs have different transfer ratios). You will need to transfer a minimum of 1,000 points.

This card has a high earnings ratio based on the two points earned on many purchases.

The American Express Gold Rewards Card also comes with Emergency Medical Insurance, including: Trip Interruption Insurance, Car Rental Theft and Damage Insurance, Lost or Stolen Baggage Insurance, Flight Delay Insurance, Hotel/Motel Burglary Insurance, and $500,000 Travel Accident Insurance.

Benefits:

- This card comes with a nice signup bonus (starts at 25,000 Membership reward points).

- No annual fee for the first year. A value of $150!

- There is no expiry or use by date on points while you stay enrolled in the Program.

- Low annual income requirements of $20,000.

- Flexible benefits (to use with frequent flyer program or other travel). Your points can even cover taxes and fees. You can also redeem points towards a travel charge up to 12 months after your trip or purchases.

- Do not need to worry about any blackouts or seat restrictions when redeeming the points.

Negatives:

- American Express is accepted at fewer locations than Visa and MasterCard, making it more difficult to use as a primary card.

- It is not possible to transfer points to someone else.

- As a Charge Card, the balance must always be paid in full each month. 30% annual interest rate applies to balances not paid in full. Payments must be received and processed by the date of the next monthly statement to avoid interest charges. This is a hefty fee but it can be avoided by using credit responsibly and paying your balance in full each month.

Starwood Preferred Guest® American Express

This is one of the best ways for Canadians to earn Starwood Preferred Guest Starpoints®. Each dollar spent earns one of the most valuable and flexible points currencies out there, Starwood Preferred Guest Starpoints®, which can be redeemed for huge value at Starwood® properties or transferred to one of nearly 30 airlines. Even better, if you transfer points in increments of 20,000, you receive a 5,000 mile bonus, which results in a net transfer ratio of one Starpoint® to 1.25 miles.

Starwood Preferred Guest® American Express Credit Card

Benefits:

- Usually a high signup bonus (ranges from 10,000 to 20,000 points).

- Receive a Free Weekend Night Award when you reach $40,000 in spending in a year.

- Free Starwood Preferred Guest Gold status when you reach $30,000 spending in a year. This status gives you free Internet, room upgrades, and late checkouts.

- Charge your airline ticket to your Starwood Preferred Guest Credit Card and receive up to $500 coverage (aggregate maximum with Baggage Delay Insurance) for hotel, motel, restaurant expenses and other sundry items.

- Book a flight with your Starwood Preferred Guest Credit Card and receive up to $500 coverage (aggregate maximum with Flight Delay Insurance) for reasonable and necessary emergency purchases.

- When you fully charge your airline tickets to your Starwood Preferred Guest Credit Card, you can receive up to $500 coverage for loss or damage to your luggage or personal effects while in transit.

- This card comes with complimentary Car Rental Theft and Damage Insurance. You will be automatically covered for damage or theft of your rental car with an MSRP of up to $85,000. To take advantage of this protection, simply decline the Loss Damage Waiver (LDW) or similar option offered by the car rental company, and fully charge your rental to your Starwood Preferred Guest Credit Card. There's no additional charge for this coverage, and you save yourself the daily insurance fee (usually $16 to $23 per day) charged by the car rental company.

Negatives:

- American Express is accepted at fewer locations than Visa and MasterCard, making it more difficult to use as a primary card.

- $50 annual fee for supplementary cards.

Capital One Aspire Travel™ World MasterCard™

This credit card was rated **The Best Travel Rewards Card** by **MoneySense Magazine** in 2012. This card is for individuals and households that have a high income, have excellent credit, and are heavy spenders.

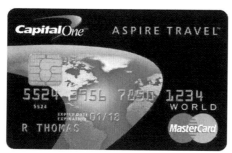

Aspire Travel World MasterCard™

The Aspire Travel World MasterCard™ offers comprehensive insurance coverage. In addition to travel accident insurance and car rental insurance, this card also offers the following insurances:

- Flight Delay: Flight delay is $250 per day up to $1000 per trip (includes you, your spouse, and your dependent children).

- Trip Interruption: Trip interruption is a maximum of $25,000 per trip (includes you, your spouse, and your dependent children).

- Trip Cancellation: Trip cancellation is a maximum of $5,000 per trip (includes you, your spouse, and your dependent children).

- Baggage Loss: $1000/trip.

- Baggage Delay: Baggage delay only up to three days (includes you, your spouse, and your dependent children).

- Price Protection: Refunds up to $100/item if a lower price is found in 60 days. Maximum of $500/year.

- Extended Warranty: Extends manufacturer's warranty for up to two additional years (typically only one year with other cards).

- Purchase Assurance: Insures most purchases against theft, loss or damage for 120 days (typically only 90 days with other cards).

This card awards two miles for every dollar spent, so the card's earnings ratio is ahead of all other Canadian travel credit cards. The card also features a nice 10,000 mile anniversary bonus for each year you renew the card.

This card lets you redeem your miles towards any expense related to your trip. Simply charge the cost of any part of the trip on the card, and go online and select your travel expense to redeem. Here is a chart that shows how the rewards earning works:

Cost of the travel	Reward Miles Required
Up to $150	15,000
$150.01 to $350	35,000
$350.01 to $600	60,000
$600.01 and greater	Travel cost × 100

One problem with this card is that you cannot use points to cover part of an expense. For example, if you spend $200 you can't use 15,000 points to cover $150 of the expense, you have to use 35,000 points.

One way around this is to split the charges if possible (ask the vendor to make two charges, $150 and $50). The tiered redemption system is a hassle, so make sure you always get the best return for your miles.

This card requires a minimum personal income of $60,000 or household income of $100,000.

Benefits:

- Double miles on all purchases.
- Can redeem your reward miles to pay for any travel-related expense (flights, hotels, car rentals, meals, and even the taxes).
- 35,000 bonus reward miles on your first purchase
- 10,000 anniversary bonus reward miles every year
- Additional users are no charge.
- Impressive insurance coverage.

Negatives:

- Confusing redemption chart with the reward tiers.
- Cannot use points to cover part of an expense.
- No way to earn miles flying.

RBC British Airways Visa Infinite

This credit card is ideally for frequent flyers who travel frequently with British Airways. You earn one Avios (British Airways frequent flyer currency) for every $1 spent on the card. With a successful application, you will earn a welcome bonus (ranging between 15,000 Avios and 50,000 depending on the time of year).

I recommend that if you want to apply for this card you wait for the promotion for the 50,000 bonus Avios points.

Benefits:

- Receive a complimentary Companion Award Ticket when you spend $30,000 or more on your card in any calendar year.
- Good overall insurances with this card including Out of Province/Country Emergency Medical Insurance, Travel Accident Group Insurance, Auto Rental Collision/Loss Damage Insurance, and Emergency Purchases and Flight Delay Insurance.

Negatives:

- High annual fee of $165.
- Not useful if you only fly domestically within Canada.

WestJet RBC World Elite MasterCard

This credit card is perfect for travelers who travel frequently in Canada and throughout North America. It is affiliated with the WestJet Rewards program, where you earn WestJet Rewards dollars for every dollar spent. This card has a $99 annual fee. This is the top credit card to earn WestJet dollars faster. Every purchase earns 1.5% back in WestJet dollars, and 2% when you purchase WestJet flights or WestJet Vacations.

This card comes with a nice suite of insurance coverage:

- Out of Province/Country Emergency Medical Insurance.

- Travel Accident Insurance

- Auto Rental Collision/Loss Damage Insurance

- Trip Interruption Insurance.

- Emergency Purchases and Flight Delay Insurance.

- Hotel/Motel Burglary Insurance

- Purchase Security and Extended Warranty Insurance.

The main attraction of this card is the welcome bonus of WestJet dollars (can be as high as $250), and an annual round-trip companion flight for $99 with your first purchase.

Benefits:

- Annual round-trip companion flight for $99 on a WestJet marketed and operated flight in Canada and the continental U.S.

- Ability to book flights with no blackout periods, extremely useful when there are no seat sales.

Negatives:

- Cannot earn rewards flying with other airlines.

- Not much choice in carrier when strictly using this card.

AeroplanPlus Platinum Card American Express

This credit card is perfect for heavy travelers and spenders in Canada. If you are concentrating on earning Aeroplan® miles, this is one of the top credit cards to have.

AeroplanPlus Platinum Card American Express

With this card you earn 1.25 Aeroplan® miles for every dollar in purchases you make up to $25,000 annually, and 1.5 Aeroplan® miles for every dollar on purchases over $25,000.

One of the nice bonuses of this card is a 2-for-1 short-haul flight reward when you redeem 15,000 Aeroplan® Miles. This could be a ticket from Vancouver to Portland, or Toronto to New York City.

This card provides free access to Air Canada Maple Leaf Lounges & Arrivals Lounges.

This card comes with a $499 annual fee. As a Charge Card, the balance must always be paid in full each month. A hefty 30% annual interest rate applies to balances not paid in full.

Benefits:

- Low minimum spending requirements.
- Annual Partner Ticket redemption bonus.
- Access to Air Canada Maple Leaf Lounges worldwide.
- Priority Check-in with Air Canada.
- Complimentary Fairmont President's Club membership.
- Access to Pearson Priority Security Lane.
- Complimentary Priority Pass Membership with access to over 600 airport lounges worldwide.
- Complimentary Hertz Rent-A-Car Gold Plus Rewards Membership and free Car Class upgrades.

- Air Canada Privilege Pass.

Negatives:

- One of the highest annual fees in Canada.

- Must be on top of paying the outstanding balance each month to prevent the hefty interest from being charged.

- Should travel frequently to make use of lounge and check in benefits.

The American Express® Platinum Card®

This is a premium charge card to own, and it comes with an annual fee of $699. This is for the traveler that wants all the perks that come with a premium charge card and enjoys travelling in first class. You require an annual personal income of at least $60,000 or more to apply for this charge card. This card usually has a high bonus for application of around 50,000. You will earn a welcome bonus (can be as high as 50,000 Membership Rewards points) by achieving minimum spending requirements.

The American Express® Platinum Card®

You earn 1.25 Membership Rewards points for every dollar in purchases charged to the Card.

This card is not affiliated with any frequent flyer program, but you have the option of transferring the Membership Reward points to other frequent flyer and hotel programs, including on a 1:1 basis to Aeroplan, Avios.

With this card, you will have a $200 Annual Travel Credit, which you can use towards any single travel booking of $200 or more charged to your Platinum Card®. This means that if you applied for the card in the middle of a year you would have $400 to use - $200 each year! The Annual Travel Credit has to be booked through Platinum Travel Service (their in-house travel agent available 24 hours a day).

Another interesting benefit of using this Platinum Card® is that when you purchase an eligible ticket with participating airlines in first class or business class, you will receive a complimentary or discounted ticket for your companion to travel with you. You will also earn complimentary seat upgrades to First Class from Business Class when travelling to destinations around the world.

The Platinum Card® offers several benefits for travellers flying from or through Toronto Pearson:

- Complimentary Valet Service at Terminal 1 and Terminal 3. The $25 Valet service fee is waived when you present your Platinum Card® upon car pick up.

- 15% Discount on parking when you use the Platinum Card® to pay for the parking at the Express Park in Terminal 1 and Daily Park in Terminals 1 and 3.

- Access to the Pearson Priority Lane when clearing security at Terminals 1 and 3.

This card also offers the following insurances:
- Emergency Medical Insurance (Out of province/country)
- Car Rental Theft Damage Insurance
- Flight Delay Insurance
- Baggage Delay Insurance
- Lost or Stolen Baggage Insurance
- Hotel/Motel Burglary Insurance
- $500,000 Travel Accident Insurance
- Travel Emergency Assistance
- Travel Medical Concierge

- Trip Cancellation Insurance
- Trip Interruption Insurance

You will also have Complimentary Membership in Priority Pass (one of the world's largest independent airport lounge programs). If you are travelling in major Canadian cities, you will receive complimentary lounge access regardless of airline or fare booked. Additionally, when traveling with participating airlines in The Airport Club Program, you can enjoy complimentary airline club access across the US and Internationally.

Benefits:

- Automatic Starwood Preferred Guest Gold, Gold Elite membership with Club Carlson, and Platinum membership with Le Club Accorhotels.
- The list of lounge access around the world included with the card is impressive.
- Flexibility to transfer to multiple programs.
- Access to Pearson Priority Lane, free Valet Parking, and discounted parking at Pearson International Airport in Toronto.

Negatives:

- One of the highest annual fees in Canada.
- $175 Annual fee for a supplement card.
- All Program bookings and purchases must be made through American Express Travel Services or at any other American Express Travel Services location in Canada to take advantage of companion fares.
- Should travel frequently to make use of high-end benefits (first-class tickets and upgrades).

TD First Class Travel Visa Infinite Card

This is a flexible travel rewards credit card, where you can redeem your travel with any provider. This credit card has an annual fee of $120. You require an annual personal income of at least $60,000 or more. You earn three TD Points for spending $1 with this credit card. If you redeemed 20,000 TD Points, you would earn $100 of travel.

This credit card includes Trip Interruption and Cancellation Coverage, Travel Medical Insurance, and Delayed and Lost Baggage Coverage.

Benefits:

- Flexible redemption by applying to any travel.
- No expiration on TD points earned.

Negatives:

- No airline partners to earn TD Points flying.
- TD Points can only be redeemed in 10,000 point increments.

American Express Blue Sky Credit Card

This is a great travel rewards credit card that has no annual fee. You earn 1.25 Blue Sky Points for every dollar in purchases. You can start redeeming with as little as 10,000 Blue Sky Points, which is worth $100 in statement credit towards any travel purchase charged to your credit card.

You will earn a welcome bonus (can be as high as 10,000 Blue Sky Points) by achieving minimum spending requirements.

Benefits:

- Flexible redemption by applying Blue Sky Points earned to any travel purchase.
- No Annual Fee.

Negatives:

- No travel partners to earn bonus miles.
- No major insurance coverage with credit card.

CIBC Aerogold Visa Infinite

With this credit card you have the ability to earn 1.5 Aeroplan miles on Grocery, Drug Store and Gas Station purchases. 150 participating Aeroplan Partners let you earn Aeroplan Miles twice when you present your Aeroplan Card. This credit card has an annual fee of $120. You require an annual personal income of at least $60,000 or more.

The card has the following insurances included:

- Out-of-Province Travel Medical Insurance for the first 15 days of a trip, for primary cardholders age 64 or under.

- Trip Interruption Insurance.
- Flight Delay and Baggage Insurance for lost, stolen, damaged or delayed checked baggage.
- Auto Rental Collision/Loss Damage Insurance.
- $500,000 Common Carrier Accident Insurance.

You will earn a welcome bonus (can be as high as 15,000 Aeroplan Miles) with your first purchase.

Benefits:

- Earn 50% more Aeroplan Miles at gas, grocery and drug stores.
- Earn up to triple the Aeroplan Miles at select CIBC Bonus Rewards establishments.
- Flexible travel options, with access to every available seat on Air Canada and Air Canada Express, including Executive Class and Executive First.
- Comprehensive insurance benefits, including Out-Of-Province Travel Medical Insurance.
- Car rental discounts of up to 25% at participating Avis and Budget locations.

Negatives:

- Cost of $50 for supplement cards.
- No major insurance coverage with credit card.

How to get your annual fee waived or reduced

Believe it or not, it's often possible to have a credit card fee waived or reduced just for asking nicely. One phone call could save you up to $100!

Here are my steps as to what you should do when you approach your anniversary date:

1. Call the toll-free customer service line on the back of your card. When you get to a prompt or speak to a customer representative, choose or ask for the card cancellation option.

2. You will be asked why you want to cancel the card. You can tell them that you cannot justify the annual fee when other credit cards available have fewer fees or none at all, while explaining that you like the card. Explain that you are a loyal customer who normally makes on-time payments. You will be told all the benefits of the card, and why it is worth the high annual fee.

3. Have the representative do all the talking at this point. They will offer a solution to you, maybe a $50 statement credit towards the annual fee or some bonus miles. If they transfer you to the retention department, they could also have an offer for you. I have done this twice for several cards of mine, and you need to make it sound like you will cancel. These companies do not want you to leave, as they spend a fortune for customer acquisition.

I wouldn't recommend threatening to cancel you card every year but these annual fees can be waived from time to time.

It doesn't hurt to try!

Tools

- Aeroplan - http://www.aeroplan.com

- Air Miles - http://www.airmiles.ca

- Asking Canadians - http://www.askingcanadians.com/

- Aeromove - http://www.aeromove.ca/

- Rocketmiles http://www.canadiantravelhacking.com/go/rocketmiles

- Audience Rewards - http://www.audiencerewards.com/

- Club Sobeys - http://www.clubsobeys.com/

- Club Thriftys - http://www.clubthriftys.com/

- Equifax Canada - http://www.equifax.ca/

- TransUnion Canada - http://www.transunion.ca/

- American Express Gold Rewards Card
  http://www.canadiantravelhacking.com/go/amex-gold

- American Express Starwood Preferred Guest - http://www.canadiantravelhacking.com/go/spg

- Capital One Aspire Travel World MasterCard - http://www.canadiantravelhacking.com/go/capitalone

- RBC British Airways Visa Infinite - http://www.canadiantravelhacking.com/go/rbc-ba

- WestJet RBC World Elite MasterCard - http://www.canadiantravelhacking.com/go/rbc-westjet

- AeroplanPlus Platinum Card American Express - http://www.canadiantravelhacking.com/go/amex-aeroplanplus

- The American Express Platinum Card - http://www.canadiantravelhacking.com/go/amex-platinum

- TD First Class Travel Visa Infinite Card - http://www.canadiantravelhacking.com/go/td-first-class

- American Express Blue Sky Credit Card - http://www.canadiantravelhacking.com/go/amex-bluesky

- CIBC Aerogold Visa Infinite - http://www.canadiantravelhacking.com/go/cibc-aerogold

Chapter 3

Using Miles

Now that you have seen all the tips and tricks that you can use to acquire frequent flyer miles, I wanted to share some of the best ways of using the miles. Each traveler's requirements are different; some want to redeem miles for a business class trip to Europe or Australia, while others may just want to take their family from Toronto to New York. This chapter will explore the best use and return for your frequent flyer miles.

Before you start to redeem your miles on any program, you should be organized. I use a free service like Awardwallet.com that lets you input and track all your frequent flyer accounts (even includes Esso, Groupon, Petro Canada, and Starbucks) in one place.

AwardWallet.com

AwardWallet provides a free service that helps you manage your reward balances and travel itineraries. The website supports 612 loyalty programs – air, hotel, car rental, credit card and others. Founded in 2004, AwardWallet quickly became a popular choice for both road warriors and casual travelers. Today, over 178,000 active members rely on AwardWallet to manage over 37.9 billion miles / points representing $758 million in value. AwardWallet is not affiliated or related to any of the loyalty programs offered by the airlines, hotels or credit cards identified on this website or tracked and monitored using the AwardWallet service.

AwardWallet.com is designed to help keeping track of different loyalty programs for you and your family. It can login on your behalf to the different reward accounts and retrieve your balance, expiration, elite level, etc. and show this information in a single, easy to understand report.

I have taken a look at each major frequent flyer program to look at the best redemptions.

Aeroplan

Aeroplan® has two levels of redemption, ClassicFlight and ClassicPlus. You can redeem your Aeroplan® miles online for free, or with their Contact Center at a cost at $30 per ticket. For complicated itineraries, I recommend calling the Contact Center. It never hurts to call the Contact Center to ask an agent for suggestions for possible flights or suggestions. I spoke to an agent who explained when it was ideal to look for inventory for ClassicFlight redemptions for a possible flight to Nunavut. The agents try their best, and sometimes they can suggest alternate routes if you cannot find inventory for the desired flights that you are looking for.

Aeroplan® has a chart that lets you find out the mileage required to redeem a ticket in each geographical area. Each chart area is broken down by ticket type (enables you to redeem an economy, business, or first class ticket at different mileage). One important note is that when flying with Air Canada Business, the top class is Business. Other Star Alliance carriers that offer First Class, the Business class ticket might offer a lower level of service than on Air Canada. I recommend looking carefully at the chart, and when you figure out your flights to contact each carrier to see the difference in redeeming miles for Business versus First Class.

From / To	Class	Cuba	Canada & Continental USA (Short-haul)	Canada & Continental USA (Long-haul)	Hawaii	Mexico	Caribbean & Central America	Northern South America	Southern South America	Europe 1	Europe 2	Asia 1	Asia 2	Middle East & North Africa	Indian Subcontinent	East, West & South Africa	Australia, New Zealand & South Pacific
Canada & Continental USA	Economy	15K	25K	45K	40K	40K	60K	90K	60K	75K	78K	90K	80K	100K	100K	90K
	Business	25K	50K	80K	80K	80K	75K	95K	90K	105K	105K	136K	105K	150K	150K	160K
	First		79K	110K	80K	80K	105K	135K	125K	145K	210K	215K	200K	210K	210K	220K
Hawaii	Economy				80K	60K	60K	50K	95K	95K	60K	86K	120K	145K	140K	60K
	Business				83K	80K	80K	80K	130K	130K	90K	90K	180K	200K	200K	90K
	First				100K	100K	110K	180K	180K	125K	126K	225K	280K	280K	125K	
Mexico	Economy					40K	50K	50K	80K	95K	100K	103K	120K	140K	140K	100K
	Business					90K	80K	80K	115K	145K	150K	150K	160K	250K	200K	160K
	First					85K	100K	110K	160K	200K	200K	200K	225K	280K	280K	200K
Caribbean & Central America	Economy						40K	50K	50K	80K	95K	103K	100K	125K	140K	140K	100K
	Business						90K	80K	80K	115K	145K	150K	150K	180K	200K	200K	150K
	First						65K	100K	110K	160K	200K	200K	200K	225K	280K	280K	200K
Northern South America	Economy							25K	40K	75K	70K	100K	100K	120K	140K	140K	175K
	Business							35K	80K	100K	100K	130K	130K	180K	200K	200K	178K
	First							85K	130K	130K	180K	180K	240K	270K	270K	220K
Southern South America	Economy								25K	80K	90K	105K	105K	120K	140K	140K	125K
	Business								40K	115K	115K	150K	150K	180K	200K	200K	178K
	First								85K	160K	180K	210K	210K	250K	280K	280K	240K
Europe 1	Economy									20K	30K	75K	75K	50K	70K	70K	100K
	Business									30K	45K	105K	105K	75K	105K	105K	145K
	First									60K	65K	145K	145K	105K	145K	145K	205K
Europe 2	Economy										30K	75K	73K	90K	70K	70K	100K
	Business										45K	105K	105K	79K	105K	105K	148K
	First										60K	145K	145K	105K	145K	145K	205K
Asia 1	Economy											20K	85K	70K	50K	140K	90K
	Business											30K	60K	115K	88K	210K	90K
	First											80K	85K	180K	120K	290K	130K
Asia 2	Economy												60K	70K	90K	140K	65K
	Business												75K	115K	85K	210K	90K
	First												120K	180K	120K	280K	130K

Aeroplan® Round-trip ClassicFlight Rewards chart.

ClassicFlight redemption

ClassicFlight awards can be booked not only with Air Canada, but with all Star Alliance member airlines. The mileage required is fixed based on the Aeroplan rewards chart.

Flight awards are capacity controlled, meaning that the available seats vary on all possible Star Alliance flights. Capacity controlled means that Air Canada offers seats that they project will not be sold. As more seats are sold on that flight, and as the flight becomes closer in time, the projection of unsold seats changes, and the number of award seats changes up or down accordingly. I recommend that if you are looking for a particular flight to check occasionally on their website for new seat availability as the date gets closer.

Within Canada and U.S.A.

Roundtrip economy class ClassicFlight awards within Canada and the U.S. are 15,000 miles for selected short-haul flights, and 25,000 miles for long-haul flights. Business class ClassicFlight awards are 25,000 miles for short-haul flights, and 50,000 miles for long-haul flights.

One of the best ways to use Aeroplan® awards is to use their short-haul flight redemption. For example, a member living anywhere in Ontario can fly for just 15,000 Aeroplan miles round-trip to Manitoba, Ontario, Quebec in Canada, and to Connecticut, Georgia, Illinois, Indiana, Maryland, Massachusetts, Michigan, Minnesota, Missouri, New Jersey, New Hampshire, New York, North Carolina, Ohio, Pennsylvania, Rhode Island, Tennessee, Virginia, Washington DC, and Wisconsin in the United States. British Columbia residents have the options of Alberta, British Columbia, Yukon, Oregon, and Washington State for a short-haul flight.

This usually means travel within your province and adjacent states and provinces. So a Thunder Bay, Ontario to New York or Whitehorse, Yukon to Vancouver, BC redemption is valid. These short-haul flights can be expensive outside of normal seat sales.

Here are some examples of some good redemption values:

1. Short-haul ticket (15,000 Aeroplan® miles).

A Victoria, BC to Whitehorse, Yukon flight can sell for upwards of $680 on Air Canada.

Air Canada flight from Victoria, BC to Whitehorse, YK.

If you were to redeem 15,000 Aeroplan® miles, dividing the fare cost by the miles redeemed ($681 / 15,000 miles), returns a value of 4.5 cents per mile.

2. Short-haul ticket (15,000 Aeroplan® miles) with a stopover.

Aeroplan® allows one free stopover even on short-haul redemptions. This is perfect for flyers who want to have a brief getaway or retreat before their final destination. For example, if you were living in Nanaimo, BC, you could fly to Vancouver, BC for a nice two-day break before your final destination in Calgary, Alberta.

If you booked this normally, it would cost you multiple tickets:

- Nanaimo to Vancouver
- Vancouver to Calgary
- Calgary to Nanaimo

On the dates chosen, this flight would have cost $653. Redeeming 15,000 Aeroplan® miles, dividing the fare cost by the miles redeemed ($653 / 15,000 miles), returns a value of 4.4 cents per mile.

Sample Air Canada itinerary.

3. Long-haul ticket in North America.

An Aeroplan® member who wants to go from St. Johns, Newfoundland to Los Angeles would pay just 25,000 Aeroplan® miles for a round-trip ticket for a flight over Christmas.

St. Johns, Newfoundland to Los Angeles, California using Aeroplan®.

My recommendation is for Canadians to travel to a part of North America as part of a free stopover on the way to their final destination to get a higher return on their redemption. If you are flying from Vancouver to St. Johns, consider a stop in Ottawa or Winnipeg to see another part of the country.

I have never been to anywhere in Canada further east than Belleville, Ontario, so one of my goals is to see more of Quebec and the Maritime provinces. Most of my trips to Ontario are to visit my friends and family in Thunder Bay and Toronto. With the stopovers available with Aeroplan®, it can become a reality for me. Here is an itinerary that lets me do a stopover in Toronto on my way to Thunder Bay, Ontario (my destination) from Victoria, BC for just 25,000 Aeroplan® miles. This ticket would normally cost close to $1,000 with taxes.

Air Canada long-haul stopover

Canada to Hawaii

Flights from Canada to Hawaii are 45,000 miles in economy and 80,000 miles in business. This is a better deal for Canadians living in Central or Eastern Canada, where they do not see many flight specials to Hawaii (unlike Calgary, Edmonton, or Vancouver).

A flight from St. Johns, Newfoundland to Honolulu, Hawaii can run over $1,000 ($1,126 in this example). I personally do not think this is the best use of Aeroplan® miles. Dividing the cost of the flight by the number of miles redeemed brings a value of just 2.5 cents per mile.

Flight from St. Johns to Honolulu, Hawaii.

Canada to Europe

Redemptions to Europe are broken down into two geographical areas, Europe 1 (Western Europe) and Europe 2 (Eastern Europe). Flights to Europe 1 from Canada are 60,000 miles round-trip and to Europe 2 are 75,000. In Business class, in Europe 1 a round-trip ticket is available for 90,000 miles and in Europe 2, it is available for 105,000 miles.

Flying within Europe is usually inexpensive, compared to flying domestically in North America, so I recommend flying to a major hub in the Europe 1 zone and looking for a low-cost fare to Europe 2.

You are allowed one stopover on your trip, but it must be a valid routing option. I suggest using the Aeroplan® website or speaking to an agent to find valid routing options for a stopover in Europe. Here is a redemption from Toronto with a stopover in Frankfurt, Germany going to Warsaw, Poland, and then returning to Toronto.

Europe 1 Aeroplan redemption.

When you select flights for each leg of your trip, look closely at the taxes for each flight. Now, this will not always work because some routes will be flown by Star Alliance partners that will have a fuel surcharge, but you can always adjust your itinerary to save some money.

Australia

An economy ticket is available for just 80,000 Aeroplan® miles. I recommend looking for flights that fly through the United States (stops in San Francisco or Los Angeles). This lets you use Air New Zealand for the longest leg of the flight. The taxes for this redemption are just $157.41.

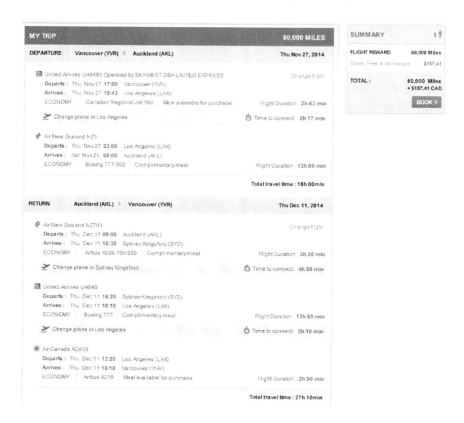

Aeroplan itinerary to Auckland, New Zealand from Canada.

Choosing a flight from a different carrier makes all the difference in the taxes paid. The main difference in this itinerary is the Air Canada return flight to Canada. This itinerary charges $500 for taxes.

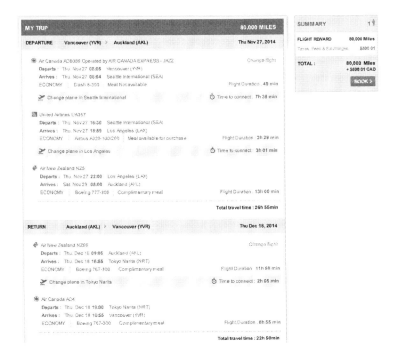

Aeroplan itinerary to Auckland, New Zealand from Canada.

However, flying to Sydney from Canada is a long trip, and can be over 24 hours of flying, so I recommend using 160,000 Aeroplan® miles to travel in Business class if you have enough Aeroplan® miles.

Asia

Like Europe, Asia is broken down into two zones, Asia 1 and Asia 2. Flights to Asia 1 from Canada are 75,000 miles round-trip, and to Asia 2 are 90,000 miles.

If I were flying to Tokyo in the Asia 1 zone, I recommend avoiding flying with Nippon Airlines and Air Canada. This flight flies through Chicago from Toronto and costs $720 with taxes.

Aeroplan Asia 1 redemption.

Using United Airlines as your carrier you would save almost $600 on your Asia 1 redemption as the taxes are just $136 for this flight.

Aeroplan Asia 1 redemption.

In Business class, in Asia 1 a round-trip ticket is available for 125,000 miles, and in Asia 2, it is available for 130,000 miles.

Like European flights, flying within Asia is usually inexpensive compared to North America. I recommend flying to a major hub in the Asia 1 zone, and looking for a low-cost fare to Asia 2.

ClassicPlus Redemption

ClassicPlus Flight Rewards offers access to a greater choice of flight departures, routes and travel times at higher mileage levels on Air Canada flights. Aeroplan® has access to any unsold seat on Air Canada flights for redemption.

One of the problems when using the ClassicPlus redemption is that the number of Aeroplan miles for the exact dates for your travel can be quite high. For a sample itinerary of Victoria, BC to Portland, Oregon, the ClassicFlight redemption would cost 15,000 Aeroplan miles. For the same itinerary, the ClassicPlus redemption would cost at a minimum 34,000 Aeroplan® miles. It is important to book your travel well in advance with Aeroplan® to make sure that you can get any ClassicFlight seats available.

Free stopovers

One of the major benefits of the ClassicFlight Aeroplan® redemptions is the generous stopover that you are allowed. In general, a stopover city is between your origin and destination.

The stopover city must be allowable within the fare rules for the origin and destination. For example, on a trip from Montreal to Vancouver, you could include a stopover in Winnipeg, but not a stopover in New York.

Here is an example of a valid Aeroplan® itinerary with a stopover within Canada. The flight goes from Halifax with a stopover in Winnipeg to Victoria and back to Halifax. This itinerary only costs 25,000 Aeroplan® miles in economy.

Sample Canadian Aeroplan® itinerary with stopover.

If you wanted to have your stopover in the United States, it is more challenging of an itinerary to put together. One of the main reasons is that you are not allowed to fly with United Airlines (one of the main carriers from Canada to the United States). You need to find an Air Canada flight to your destination, and these are usually only available from major airports like Vancouver, Montreal, and Toronto.

If you were flying to Honolulu in Hawaii from Toronto, you could add a free stopover in Vancouver at a total cost of 45,000 Aeroplan miles to travel in economy. The flight goes from Toronto with a stopover in Vancouver to Honolulu, Hawaii, and back to Toronto.

Sample Hawaii Itinerary on Aeroplan®.

Here is another itinerary that starts in Toronto and has a stopover in Portland, Oregon, with a trip to Vancouver, BC and back to Toronto for 25,000 Aeroplan® miles.

Sample US Itinerary on Aeroplan®.

Here are the rules for stopovers between zones:

Travel Zones	Rule
Travel within Canada or between Canada and the Continental USA (not including Hawaii/Puerto Rico)	*One stopover permitted in addition to the point of turnaround except on any itinerary that includes a United Airlines flight.*
Travel between Canada/Continental USA and Hawaii/Puerto Rico/Mexico/Central America/Caribbean	*For rewards containing only Air Canada flights, two stopovers are permitted in addition to the point of turnaround. One open jaw is permitted in lieu of one stopover.*
	For rewards containing a minimum of one flight on a Star Alliance partner other than Air Canada, one stopover is permitted in addition to the point of turnaround. One open jaw is permitted in addition to the one stopover.
Travel between two continents	*Two stopovers are permitted in addition to the point of turnaround. One open jaw is permitted in lieu of one of the two stopovers.*

These stopovers are a major value, and save you from redeeming extra Aeroplan miles for multiple flights.

Best value is to fly business class

My strong recommendation if you are looking for the best redemption value is to save your Aeroplan® miles for a business class ticket. These tickets are very expensive, and can be at least four-five times the price of an economy ticket.

A flight inside North America using a business class ticket is not the best value. I feel that the distance is not long enough to pay the extra Aeroplan® miles to fly business class. Flying internationally with business class is a better return, not just for the extra leg room but meals, lounge access, easier security lines, and baggage allowance. You ultimately need to decide whether you personally value business travel enough to pay the extra mileage required.

Here is a sample business ticket price from Vancouver to London Heathrow that costs $7,035, using the ITA Matrix.

Itinerary

Vancouver (YVR) to London (LHR) - Mon, Dec 1
Vancouver (YVR) to Chicago (ORD) - Mon, Dec 1
Air Canada 5132   Dep: 11:00AM   Arr: 5:02PM   4h 2m   Airbus A320   Business (Z)
OPERATED BY UNITED   Layover in ORD   1h 48m
AIRLINES, INC.

Chicago (ORD) to London (LHR) - Mon, Dec 1
American Airlines Inc. 86 Dep: 6:50PM   Arr: 8:35AM   7h 45m   Boeing 777   First (P)
Tue, Dec 2

London (LHR) to Vancouver (YVR) - Tue, Dec 9
London (LHR) to Chicago (ORD) - Tue, Dec 9
American Airlines Inc. 87 Dep: 10:15AM   Arr: 1:10PM   8h 55m   Boeing 777   First (P)
Layover in ORD   2h 0m

Chicago (ORD) to Vancouver (YVR) - Tue, Dec 9
Air Canada 5133   Dep: 3:10PM   Arr: 5:51PM   4h 41m   Airbus A319   Business (Z)
OPERATED BY UNITED
AIRLINES, INC.

Cost per passenger (including taxes & fees)   CA$7,035.21
Total cost for 1 passenger   **CA$7,035.21**

Sample Business Class Itinerary

If you booked your reward using your Aeroplan® miles, it would cost 90,000 miles. The main reason why this redemption is a good return is that the flight from Vancouver is over 9 hours and it is not fun travelling in economy for a long flight. Dividing the cost of the flight ($7,035) by the number of miles redeemed (90,000) brings a value of 7.8 cents.

Booking early is important

Aeroplan® will allow you to book reward travel up to 355 days in advance. This is important to remember on high-demand routes to Australia and Asia, and for most types of business or First class tickets.

Round-the-world ticket

Aeroplan® has a round-the-world ticket for redeeming 200,000 Aeroplan® miles for an Economy ticket, and 300,000 for First Class.

Here are the rules involved with booking this kind of ticket:

1. A maximum of five stopovers and one open jaw are permitted per flight reward on eligible routings. Only one stopover is permitted in any one city.

2. Travel must commence from and return to the same country, and return cannot go beyond the point of origin.

3. Flight reward must include one transatlantic and one transpacific crossing.

You have five stops, so this lets you fly Toronto to Buenos Aires to Bangkok to Istanbul to Paris to New York back to Toronto. When booking round-the-world tickets or multiple stopovers (more than one), you will need to call the Aeroplan® contact center, as their website's multi city tool only lets you input two cities.

Mini round-the-world ticket

The redemption of an Aeroplan® mini round the world ticket (allowed two stops and a point of turnaround) is a real bargain. Aeroplan® allows you to route one leg of an Asian ticket across the Pacific with a stopover in a European city and the other across the Atlantic, effectively giving you an around-the-world itinerary. This allows you to get the best return on your Aeroplan® miles.

Here is a sample itinerary for a flight that begins and ends in Toronto. For a cost of 75,000 Aeroplan® miles (Asia 1 reward in Economy) you could fly from Toronto to Hong Kong (Asian hub city) with a stopover in Frankfurt (European hub city), and then return to Toronto. This gets you overseas, over the Pacific, and lets you return via the Atlantic.

This Mini round-the-world itinerary has a cost of 75,000 Aeroplan miles in Economy.

I recommend using 70,000 more Aeroplan® miles for a Business class ticket for a total of 150,000 Aeroplan® miles. This lets you travel in Business/First class the entire trip, and gives you access to the airport lounges (usually free with a Business or First Class ticket)!

Tips:

1. Try to fly into Star Alliance™ hub cities in both continents to give you more direct flight options.

2. Try to avoid airlines that charge extra for a fuel surcharge.

3. If you want to redeem more Aeroplan miles within a geographical area, you can still have a free stopover. For travel within Aeroplan® zone Europe 1, you could fly from Frankfurt to Vienna with a stopover in Zurich back to Frankfurt for an additional cost of 20,000 Aeroplan® miles in Economy.

4. On short intra-Asia or intra-Europe flights, there is not much advantage to flying in business or first class, due to the short duration of the flights.

5. The only major restriction is the total distance that you want to travel, which is a maximum of 25,000 miles.

Avoiding hefty taxes

Aeroplan's airline partners determine whether or not to apply fuel surcharges. Aeroplan® is required to collect these charges on applicable rewards tickets on behalf of its airline partners.

Here is an example of an Aeroplan® redemption for an economy class ticket from Montreal to Zurich for 60,000 Aeroplan miles.

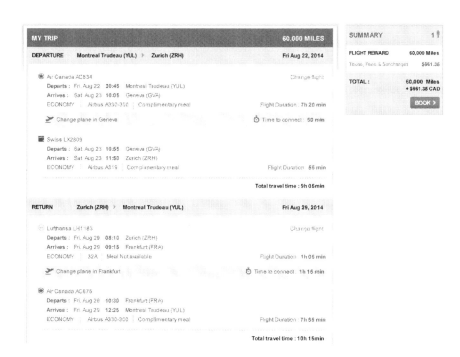

Aeroplan itinerary Montreal to Zurich.

Flying with Air Canada and Swiss Air, the total airport taxes, fees, and surcharges are $661.

Airport Taxes, Fees & Surcharges	Close ✕
	Adult(s)
Swiss Passenger Security and Noise Charge	$88.30
Fuel Surcharge	$476.00
Nav Canada - Air Navigation Services	$30.00
Canada Domestic/International Airport Improvement Fee	$25.00
Canada Goods And Service Tax	$1.25
Canada Quebec Sales Tax	$2.49
Canada Domestic/International Air Travel Security Charge	$25.91
Germany International Passenger Service Charge	$32.40
Total per passenger	$661.35
Total passengers	1
	$661.35
Total airport taxes, fees and surcharges (CAD)	$661.35

Total airport taxes, fees and surcharges for Montreal to Geneva, Business Class.

If you were to book the same flight on Aeroplan with another carrier, United Airlines for the flight to Zurich, and using Swiss Air for the return flight to Montreal, the taxes, fees, and surcharges would be only $129.

Aeroplan itinerary Montreal to Zurich.

The main difference is the lack of a fuel surcharge on the carriers Swiss Air and United Airlines in the Star Alliance. Using this itinerary would save you $532, enough for a few short-haul tickets in Europe.

Total airport taxes, fees and surcharges for Montreal to Geneva, Business Class.

If you want to avoid high fuel surcharges on rewards flights, I recommend that you attempt to use your Aeroplan® miles for flights on other Star Alliance carriers, which don't impose fuel surcharges or charge less.

With any Aeroplan® reward ticket, you will be responsible for paying all fees and taxes that would be applicable on a standard revenue ticket.

Aeroplan® redemptions for infants

Whatever you choose, your mileage redemption or flat fee will be the same across infant ticket travel zones:

- Economy Class - $50 or 5,000 Aeroplan® Miles
- Business Class - $100 or 10,000 Aeroplan® Miles
- First Class - $125 or 12,500 Aeroplan® Miles

AIR MILES®

AIR MILES has two reward streams: Cash Rewards and Dream Rewards. Dream Rewards are redemption options like merchandise or flights and travel. Cash Rewards are accumulated at the same rate as regular AIR MILES. With Cash Rewards, once you have 95 AIR MILES, you can redeem for $10 at the check-out of participating Sponsors like Metro, Shell and RONA, up to $750 per day. I value an AIR MILE using the Cash Rewards redemption, by earning at the base fare, at 10.5 cents (95 AIR MILES / $10) unless Collectors accumulate more reward miles through ongoing Bonus offers.

AIR MILES Dream flight redemptions are distance based using a zone to zone structure. Based on the flight map for redemptions, an AIR MILES flight from Victoria, British Columbia to Calgary, Alberta would cost 1,025 AIR MILES for a round-trip ticket in the low season. A flight booked with WestJet costs approximately $350 for a round-trip ticket for the same itinerary. If you were to redeem the same number of AIR MILES for a Cash Reward, it would give you a return of just over $100 (95 AIR MILES * $10). The return on each reward mile with this flight redemption is 34 cents ($350 / 1,025 AIR MILES).

To get the best return on your AIR MILES, look for routes that are normally expensive. Flying during the high season is expensive with the AIR MILES required for redemption. If you plan on using this as your main loyalty program, you should apply for the BMO Bank of Montreal AIR MILES World MasterCard®. All cardholders get a 25% discount off the regular price in AIR MILES for flights. So, for example, instead of redeeming 1,025 AIR MILES for a flight between Vancouver to Calgary, you would only need 768 AIR MILES.

AIR MILES allows you to book your travel online, but note that online bookings are subject to a service fee of $15.00 (plus applicable taxes) per ticket. Bookings made through the Customer Care Centre are subject to a service fee of $30.00 (plus applicable taxes) per ticket.

Look carefully at the Flight Map

I do see some high AIR MILES redemption costs between some areas in Canada. For example, a flight between Victoria, British Columbia (Zone 1) and Toronto, Ontario (Zone 5) costs 3,125 AIR MILES. This flight usually costs around $600 with taxes, so the return is 19 cents per mile. This is an example where the Dream AIR MILES redemption is better than the Cash Rewards redemption, but still not the best return for your miles.

Another example is a flight from Vancouver, British Columbia, to Sydney, Australia during the AIR MILES redemption high season (between December 16 and January 7). This flight can cost as little as $1,600.

The AIR MILES redemption for this flight would cost 15,550 AIR MILES. This would give you a return of 10.2 cents per mile ($1,600 / 15,550 AIR MILES). Unless you can find a good AIR MILES return, I recommend sticking to the simpler Cash Rewards redemption.

Beware the fuel surcharges

By agreement with the airlines, the AIR MILES Reward Program purchases airline tickets to which fuel surcharges and other fees and taxes apply. In order to make flight rewards attainable by the average Collector, the AIR MILES Reward Program has set the number of miles required to be redeemed as equivalent to the base fare, excluding surcharges and taxes, which the Collector pays in cash.

Watch for their redemption specials

Occasionally, AIR MILES will show promotions where you can save anywhere between 10 to 25 percent on the AIR MILES required for the redemption. You can find these promotions in the Travel area in the Dream Rewards section of the AIR MILES website.

Become a Gold member

If you are looking at redeeming AIR MILES, I recommend becoming a Gold member. The AIR MILES Gold program provides members with exclusive benefits, including flight and merchandise discounts, and Gold-only Sponsor Bonus Offers. You can automatically become an AIR MILES Gold member when you earn 1,000 AIR MILES in a calendar year and shop at five different AIR MILES Sponsors.

If you were looking to take a flight reward at 1,000 miles and own the BMO AIR MILES World MasterCard, which qualifies you for the 25% discount on flight redemptions, it would only cost you 750 reward miles. You can also find savings of up to 40% off reward miles required for select flights from the Deals of the Week offers updated every Monday on their website.

Package Vacations

AIR MILES lets you redeem your AIR MILES with various Canadian vacation providers such as Beaches Resorts, Club Med, Contiki Holidays, G Adventures, Horizon Holidays, Insight Vacations, Sandals Resorts, Sunquest Vacations, Trafalgar Tours, Transat Holidays, WestJet Vacations and with a variety of Cruise lines.

You do not have any option to book these rewards on the AIR MILES website. You will need to speak to a Package Vacation and Cruise Specialist. In speaking with an agent over the phone, I was told that they do not publish the redemption rates for vacation packages. The agent did tell me that a value of $1,000 of vacation is valued at approx. 7,000 AIR MILES (giving you a return of 14.2 cents per mile). They also charge a booking fee, but this is a good option if you have miles saved but cannot find a flight to redeem with. AIR MILES also allows the ability for its Collectors to redeem only a portion of their reward miles towards Package Vacations and Cruise bookings, and then pay the rest.

Alaska Airlines®

The Alaska Airlines® mileage program allows frequent fliers to use miles to book flights on the airline's own network or on flights with any of Alaska's partner airlines.

An economy fare on Alaska Airlines® will cost 25,000 miles for a return ticket. If you fly from a Canadian city to Miami or Boston or New York, this is a good return on your miles, as these flights can be expensive.

One of the major benefits of this program is the redemption flexibility with partners like Cathay Pacific, American Airlines, Delta, and Qantas.

On a past redemption, I used just 80,000 Alaska Airlines® miles to redeem with partner American Airlines® to take my wife, daughter, and myself to Europe in low season (October 15 - May 15). I thought it was a great return on our miles because we split our trip into a few trips with stopovers. We initially flew from Seattle, Washington to Newark, New Jersey for a stopover, and flew from New York City (JFK) to London Heathrow. On the return, we flew from London to New York City, and then returned to Seattle. The stopover in Newark worked well, as we split up the trip to fly to Florida on a seat sale, and we got to spend some time in New York City.

If you used Aeroplan for this redemption, the cost would have been 150,000 Aeroplan miles.

During high season (May 16 - Oct. 14), 60,000 miles are required for each ticket, as opposed to 40,000. A business first/class ticket would be 100,000 miles.

Another interesting redemption with American Airlines using Alaska Airlines® miles are for flights to South America. A coach ticket to Deep South America would be 40,000 miles in low season (March 1 - May 31 and August 16 - November 30), and 60,000 miles in high season (December 1 - February 29 and June 1 - August 15).

Alaska charges a $15 ticketing fee per award reservation booked by phone, and a $25 partner award fee for redemptions that involve one of their airline partner airlines. The calls to book travel with their partners can be complicated, and can take several calls to find the right itinerary and available seats.

Alaska does waive the phone ticketing fee for their MVP Gold and MVP Gold 75K members. However, everyone has to pay the partner award fee if traveling on one of their partner airlines.

Another major benefit of redeeming with Alaska Airlines is the sheer number of partners they have like American Airlines, Delta Air Lines, Air France, Cathay Pacific, Emirates, Fiji Airways, KLM, and Qantas. Alaska Airlines allows one stopover of more than 24 hours or one open jaw on international awards. Given that you can't mix airlines on an award ticket, this typically translates to a stopover in the partner airlines' hub city.

We are planning to go to New Zealand in 2015, and the redemption we have planned is to take Cathay Pacific from Vancouver to Hong Kong (their hub as our free stopover).

British Airways Avios

Avios points are the currency of the British Airways frequent flyer program, the Executive Club. The price you pay for your flight will depend on which zone your destination is in, and you can choose to pay full Avios or a combination of Avios and cash. In addition to the full Avios or Avios and cash, you will also need to pay taxes, fees, and carrier charges unless you are purchasing a reward flight saver booking. A destination's zone depends on the distance between the departure city and the destination city. The further away a destination is, the higher the zone.

The table below shows the full Avios price, and where shown, the additional taxes, fees, and carrier charges, for a return flight for each zone.

Zone	Avios
Zone 1	9,000 + taxes, fees and carrier charges
Zone 2	15,000 + taxes, fees and carrier charges
Zone 3	20,000 + taxes, fees and carrier charges
Zone 4	25,000 + taxes, fees and carrier charges
Zone 5	40,000 + taxes, fees and carrier charges
Zone 6	50,000 + taxes, fees and carrier charges
Zone 7	60,000 + taxes, fees and carrier charges
Zone 8	70,000 + taxes, fees and carrier charges
Zone 9	100,000 + taxes, fees and carrier charges

Avios zone chart.

The British Airways mileage program has its perks and allows you to redeem the Avios miles with its partner airlines, such as American Airlines, Cathay Pacific, or Alaska Airlines. Redemption inventory usually opens up 355 days prior to departure. Bookings can be made up to 24 hours before departure.

The program is also based on the segments of flights for redemption. If you were flying from Vancouver, British Columbia to Seattle, Washington and then flying to Los Angeles, California, it would be two Avios redemptions.

Short-haul tickets

The Avios program uses the distance of the flight to calculate how many points are needed. Flights 650 miles or under are only 4,500 Avios each way in economy. For just 4,500 Avios miles, you could fly from Toronto to Chicago, or Toronto to New York City (9,000 Avios roundtrip). Using Aeroplan miles, this redemption would cost 15,000 Aeroplan miles for a trip to New York City and Chicago would be 25,000 Aeroplan miles, so this is a good value.

About your flights

9,000 Avios to fly from Toronto to Chicago.

To purchase the same flight itinerary, it would cost around $400. This redemption gives you a return of 4.4 cents per Avios point ($400 / 9,000).

Toronto to Chicago return flight.

Most redemptions for domestic flights within North America cost 25,000 miles with the various frequent flyer programs. Avios has some good values for shorter distance flights with its partners American Airlines and Alaska Airlines.

Here are some good value redemptions with Avios:

- Vancouver, BC (YVR) to Los Angeles, CA (LAX), 15,000 Avios

- Toronto, ON (YYZ) to Miami, FL (MIA), 20,000 Avios

- Victoria, BC (YYJ) to Seattle, WA (SEA), 9,000 Avios

- Calgary, AB (YYC) to Dallas, TX (DFW) 20,000 Avios

- Edmonton, AB (YEG) to Seattle, WA (SEA) 9,000 Avios

Avios and Cash Redemptions

When booking flights using British Airways, on some routes you will be given an option to use a combination of Avios and cash.

One example of how this works is that a typical flight from Victoria, British Columbia to Seattle, Washington would cost 9,000 Avios for a return ticket. Instead of using 9,000 Avios, you have the option of using 4,500 Avios and $70 to pay for the return ticket. This gives you a return of over 7 cents on each Avios.

Using $70 saves you from using 4,500 Avios, so you are acquiring each Avios for just 1.5 cents. This flight is usually between $350 and $400 return. If you are planning on using Avios for an economy ticket, look at this redemption option.

Transatlantic Flights

It is important to save money not just on redemptions, but on taxes also. British Airways doesn't charge fuel surcharges on Aer Lingus flights (a partner airline). A nice route to get to Europe is from Boston to Dublin on Aer Lingus, with the redemption of only 25,000 Avios roundtrip in coach or 50,000 Avios for business class.

Caribbean

A flight from Canada to the Caribbean can be expensive with most frequent flyer programs as redemptions with Aeroplan cost 40,000 Aeroplan miles to the Caribbean. Using partner American Airlines, a flight from Toronto, Ontario to New York (JFK) costs just 9,000 Avios. From JFK Airport to the island of St. Thomas in the United States Virgin Islands is 20,000 Avios return. For a grand total of 29,000 Avios redeemed, you can fly to the Carribean round trip!

American Airlines also flies to destinations like the island of Saint Kitts, serving the nation of Saint Kitts and Nevis, Barbados, and Curacao.

Flights to the Caribbean can typically be very expensive. This route typically can cost around $800. This will give you an average redemption value of 2.75 cents/point – not as good as some of the other redemptions, but not bad! You have to remember that this redemption is two trips, so you can have a nice getaway in New York City included.

Watch for transfer bonuses

Occasionally, you will see promotions from other frequent flyer programs like Starwood to transfer points to Avios. So instead of the regular 25% transfer bonus, you would receive another 25%. If you transferred 20,000 SPG points, you would get 31,250 Avios.

US Airways

US Airways' frequent flyer program has some incredible bargains for redemptions to the Caribbean, Europe, and South America during off-peak times.

You can find US Airways flights from Canada departing from Halifax, Quebec City, Montreal, Ottawa, Toronto, Edmonton, Calgary, and Vancouver.

Here is the complete US Airways off-season award travel chart:

US Airways off-peak award travel chart.

To fly to Europe with Aeroplan will cost 60,000 Aeroplan miles return. The main reason I recommend that people join the Starwood rewards program (SPG) is due to redemption rewards like these. SPG allows you to transfer your Starwood points to most other frequent flyer programs. An off-peak redemption to Europe with US Airways redemption saves you from using 25,000 miles.

American Airlines

American Airlines, with its AAdvantage frequent flyer program, has some great redemption values and policies for stopovers. This is another transfer partner of Starwood Preferred Guest.

Off-peak date redemption

If you are comfortable redeeming your frequent flyer miles in the off-season, you can find some great values for popular destinations. For example, the Europe redemption has seven months of off-peak availability at a cost of 40,000 AAdvantage miles.

Here is the current AAdvantage off-peak redemption chart with destinations, the off-peak period, and the miles required for a return ticket in economy.

Destination	Off-peak Period	Miles Required
Hawaii	January 12 - March 13; August 22 - December 15	35,000
The Caribbean and Mexico	September 7 - November 14	25,000
Central America, Colombia, Ecuador, Peru, and Venezuela	January 16 - June 14; September 7 – November 14	30,000
Argentina, Bolivia, Brazil, Chile, Paraguay, and Uruguay	March 1 - May 31; August 16 - November 30	40,000
Europe	October 15 - May 15	40,000
Japan and Korea	October 1 - April 30	50,000

Tools

- Award Wallet- http://www.awardwallet.com/

- Aeroplan - http://www.aeroplan.ca/

- Air Miles - http://www.airmiles.ca/

- Alaska Airlines® - http://www.alaskaairlines.com/

- British Airways Avios - http://www.ba.com/

- US Airways - http://www.usairways.com/

- Flying Blue - http://www.flyingblue.com/

- American Airlines - http://www.aa.com/

Chapter 4

Canadian Air Travel Hacks

Domestic air travel within Canada is expensive. We do not have as much competition between routes, and only two major airlines compete across Canada. Our country is not like Europe, where several major cities are in a small area. In Canada, foreign carriers are not allowed to compete on routes within Canada.

I am going to show some tips and tricks on how to save money on air travel with some travel hacking!

Create a free price alert

If you have flexibility with your travelling dates, or have a set budget in mind, I recommend creating a free price alert that sends you an email when your desired itinerary is available.

This is really easy with Kayak.com. Simply search for your desired flight itinerary and on the left side of the page, click the Price Alert hyperlink. After clicking on the hyperlink, a popup box will appear asking for your Price Alert parameters. You can define the maximum price that you are willing to pay for a return ticket, and your preference for number of stops and times.

Price Alert parameters.

Look for a promo code

The three main airlines in Canada are Air Canada, Westjet, or Porter (based in Toronto Island). What happens is that one airline will have a sale or promo code for certain itineraries. The other airlines will always match the promotion with a code of their own.

When redeeming the promo codes, remember that the discount is only off the base fare (before taxes, fees, fuel surcharges) and not on the total price. Also, it is not uncommon for the airlines to raise their prices first before offering a discount promo code, making it a marketing gimmick, rather than an actual savings.

Use a travel aggregator

Websites, like Kayak.com, Expedia, or Travelocity, allow you to search fares from numerous airline websites and other travel websites for a desired route.

My favourite website to use is Kayak.com. The results screen has many filters and options. You can order results by price, duration, or number of stops. You can choose to see only nonstops, only flights by certain carriers, and exclude certain connecting airports. Remember that not all airlines allow their fares to be listed (Porter Airlines, for instance, is not on Kayak.com).

I wanted to show an example of how I use these websites to save money. I am looking for the lowest economy seat from Toronto Pearson to London Heathrow.

Using Kayak.com, I enter my search criteria and receive a quote of $1,241 with Luftansa.

Sample search with Kayak.com

After you receive your first set of results, try other aggregator websites like Skyscanner.ca or Momondo.com to see if they could beat the price. These two are my favorite, as they tend to search a wider range of booking sites as well as discount airline carriers.

The same flight on Skyscanner returned at $1,217.

Skyscanner search

Now that we have found that Aer Lingus has the lowest fare, we will head directly to their website to see if we can get the fare for even less. Sometimes you will find a cheaper fare on the airlines own website than on the aggregator website, as the airlines want to entice people to book directly. Checking on the Aer Lingus website, we see that the price is even less, $1,185.

Aer Lingus search.

If flying internationally, try another currency

It pays sometimes to check if the fare is cheaper in another currency. So if I choose the Alitalia website (Alitalia.com) I will see the Canadian prices for flights because I am based in Canada.

The price in Canadian is $1,331.76 on Alitalia.com.

Alitalia.com ticket cost.

However, if I visit Alitalia.fr, the price of the fare in Euros is €873,28.

Alitalia.com ticket cost.

Even at the current exchange rate of 1.34 Euros to $1 Canadian you will still save money.

Student Discounts

International Student Identity Card (ISIC)

ISIC can provide discounts for travel (flights, train) and attractions such as museums. It is the only internationally recognized proof of full-time student status in the world, and is a student travel discount card in 70 countries worldwide, including Canada.

If travelling abroad, the ISIC provides discounts on accommodation, admission to historical sites and museums, and transportation. The price of the ISIC is $20. For full-time students who are members of either the Canadian Federation of Students or the Canadian Federation of Students-Service, the card is issued as a benefit of membership, and the $20 fee is waived.

Travel CUTS

As Canada's only national student travel bureau, Travel CUTS provides unique student-oriented products and services to over 300,000 students each year. Travel CUTS staff offer a wealth of information with years of collective student travel knowledge.

Through the Federation's membership in the International Student Travel Confederation, Travel CUTS is affiliated with over 600 student travel offices. This relationship allows Travel CUTS to negotiate and provide international student products, such as a worldwide network of student fares on air and surface transportation, the International Student Identity Card (ISIC), and student travel insurance.

Air Canada Student Pass

Air Canada offers commuting Canadian students the Air Canada Student Pass. This affordable and flexible Pass is available as a package of six one-way flight credits on Tango fares, for one traveler. It ensures complimentary advance seat selection, and accumulation of Aeroplan Miles, as well as 24/7 online booking.

Group Discounts

Travelling as a group on business, or for a school function, athletic event, wedding, or family reunion? Air Canada and WestJet offer competitive rates for groups of 10 or more people travelling together on the same date to the same destination. You need to fill out a form with the airline's group desk to request a special rate.

Here are some of the group discount benefits with Air Canada:

- Advance seating
- Flexible payment and ticketing terms
- Complimentary tickets (based on the number of ticketed passengers)

Try an alternative airport

Travelling in Canada can be expensive, however, if you are willing to drive to your closest United States border city, you can find less expensive airports to fly out of.

You can even save time by flying from the United States if your final destination is within the United States. If you fly from Canada to the United States, it is considered an international flight, which requires you to arrive several hours prior to departure.

Here is a sample flight for a fictional family of four: two adults and two children over the age of two, looking to travel from Vancouver, British Columbia to Hawaii.

Scenario 1:

For a flight leaving Vancouver (YVR) to Waikiki (HNL), it would cost $3,487.48. This was found using the ITA Matrix and using the lowest cost for a date.

ITA Matrix search from Vancouver to Honolulu round-trip flight.

Scenario 2:

Flying out of Bellingham, Washington (a city one hour drive south of the US border) would cost $1,604.80 with debit or $1,636.80 with your credit card. This is a savings of $1,850.

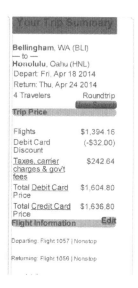

Discount airline booking from US carrier, Allegiant.

Here are some other airports to consider for your next holiday:

- Bangor, Maine (BGR)
- Presque Isle, Maine (PQI)
- Detroit, Michigan (DTW)
- Sault Ste. Marie, Michigan (CIU)
- Minneapolis, Minnesota (MSP)
- Great Falls, Montana (GTF)
- Kalispell, Montana (FCA)
- Buffalo, New York (BUF)
- Niagara Falls, New York (IAG)
- Plattsburgh, New York (PBG)
- Syracuse, New York (SYR)

- Watertown, New York (ART)
- Fargo, North Dakota (FAR)
- Grand Forks, North Dakota (GFK)
- Burlington, Vermont (BTV)
- Bellingham, Washington (BLI)
- Seattle, Washington (SEA)
- Spokane, Washington (GEG)

The cost to cross the international border may exceed the comparative cost of the plane ticket directly from Canada, so I recommend doing the math on a case-by-case basis.

Other costs to consider that should factor into your decision include:

- Fuel costs (how fuel efficient is your vehicle?)
- Parking your vehicle at the airport
- Cost of hotel if it requires an overnight stay
- Driving Time
- Vehicle Depreciation

Lowest Possible Price on Air Canada

Air Canada has a free service called **Fare Alerts**. You just put in your desired itinerary and set your budget, and they will let you know via email as soon as a fare reaches or drops below that mark. They scan fare prices available over the next two months at aircanada.com.

Fare Alerts are available for travel to or from cities across Canada, the U.S., Mexico, and the Caribbean.

webSaver weekly deals

Air Canada has a free email service that sends you exclusive offers, seat sale fares, vacation packages, car and hotel deals, travel tips, and more.

Learn to navigate the website

Before you start searching for your flights, take a close look at the website, and check the right-hand column for deals.

Air Canada website.

Air Canada highlights promotions and coupon codes on the right side of the page, so it is worth it to check out prior to booking your travel plans.

Air Canada Lowest Price Guarantee

If, within 24 hours after completing a purchase on aircanada.com or aircanada.com/agent, you find a price for the exact same Air Canada flight that's at least $5 less, Air Canada will offer you a credit of $50 plus the price difference, per passenger.

You'll receive your Air Canada Lowest Price Guarantee credit in the form of a promotion code, which you can then easily apply toward a future travel purchase on aircanada.com or aircanada.com/agent.

Last Minute Upgrade Purchase

Did you know that when you check in online, on your mobile device, or at a self-service Check-in Kiosk, on an Air Canada flight that you could be offered a Last Minute Upgrade Purchase to the Executive cabin.

Some of the advantages of Executive travel, include:

- priority security clearance
- priority boarding
- access to the Maple Leaf Lounge at the airport from which your upgraded flight segment departs

- lie-flat beds on most international flights
- premium wines, spirits and cuisine

What you need to know is that the price of the Last Minute Upgrade is based on the flight segment for which the upgrade is being selected and for flights operated by Air Canada or Jazz departing from Canada or United States.

A Last Minute Upgrade Purchase is not available for:

- Air Canada codeshare flights or flights operated by other airlines;
- Bookings with more than one passenger, if one of the passengers does not want to purchase an upgrade
- Bookings with more than one passenger, when not all the passengers can be confirmed in the Executive cabin.

Find the lowest price on Westjet

Use JetMail

JetMail keeps you informed about low fares and great travel deals with WestJet on their North American, Central American and Caribbean network. Their regular email updates contain valuable information on seat sales, special offers, exciting destinations, and useful travel tips for an enjoyable flying experience.

You can also sign up to receive a dedicated WestJet Vacations email with the latest vacation package offers, news, and destinations.

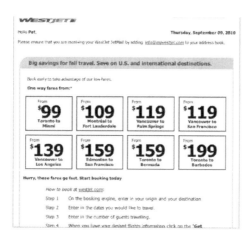

Sample WestJet JetMail.

WestJet Blue Tag

WestJet is active on social media with a presence on Facebook and Twitter. They post new Blue Tag deals with a Facebook update or via a tweet as soon as an offer is announced. This usually starts at 1 p.m. Mountain time and goes until 4 p.m.

Here is what you need to know:

- The promotion changes every week.
- Fares are valid for new bookings only, and can only be made on westjet.com.
- All fares are based on availability on select travel days as outlined in each promotion.
- Blue Tag will not occur if there is an existing seat sale.
- Unless otherwise indicated, a promo code isn't necessary.
- Blue Tag fares disappear as soon as the promotion expires.

Consider Sunwing

Sunwing is a low cost airline that offers holiday packages from Canada to the Caribbean, Central America, Mexico, Europe, and the U.S.A. They also have seasonal flights within Canada (usually during the summer) from Vancouver to Toronto and Toronto to St. Johns, with some great prices. For a sample itinerary from Toronto to Vancouver in June 2014, I found a price of $441 (including tax) for a round-trip economy ticket.

Airline Flight No	Departing City	Departing Date & Time	Arriving City	Arriving Date & Time	Price (CAD)
Sunwing Airlines WG801	Toronto (YYZ)	Wed. Jun 18, 2014 8:30 pm	Vancouver (YVR)	Wed. Jun 18, 2014 10:35 pm	$441
Sunwing Airlines WG802	Vancouver (YVR)	Sun. Jun 22, 2014 10:35 pm	Toronto (YYZ)	Mon. Jun 23, 2014 6:05 am	(Round trip) Includes taxes and fees

Sample Sunwing booking.

All Sunwing flights include hot towel service, a hot meal or hot snack depending on flight time, wine with hot meals, soft drinks, and complimentary in-flight entertainment, including first run movies.

Use a cash-back website to get a rebate

Do you search and book your best deals via websites like Hotwire or Expedia? Access them through a cash-back shopping website and get a rebate.

You basically log on to the cash-back website before heading over to the retailer's website. Cashback amounts are automatically calculated at checkout, and cheques are sent every quarter.

Two of my favourite cash-back shopping websites for Canadians are Great Canadian Rebates and Ebates.

Great Canadian Rebates Homepage.

Fly into an alternate airport

If you are flying into Miami and the flights are too expensive, consider flying into an alternate airport like Fort Lauderdale. I have done this in the past, successfully saving money. Instead of flying into JFK directly into New York, I flew into Newark in New Jersey, and took a shuttle to New York City.

The website AlternateAirports.com shows alternate airports with the driving miles between the airports denoted.

Save nearly 50% in business class

Many airlines in conjunction with their frequent flyer program will have promotions on the sale of their frequent flyer miles.

Starwood has a semi-annual promotion to save 25% when purchasing between 13,000 and 20,000 Starpoints. A purchase of 20,000 points would cost $525.00 or 2.6 cents per point. However, Starwood provides a 5,000 point bonus when transferring to another program, so including the bonus miles in the calculation, the points cost 2.1 cents per point.

The key here is finding redemptions that are worth more than 2.1 cents per point. A return business class ticket redemption for Aeroplan costs 75,000 Aeroplan miles. If you were to transfer all your Starpoints that are purchased to Aeroplan, you would pay $1,575.00.

A return business class ticket for an Air Canada flight can range from as low as $3,000 to well over $4,000. If you are looking at flying business class, I recommend seriously looking at purchasing miles during promotions to get the best redemption rates.

Price Protection

If you enjoy booking all-inclusive holidays, and you book a qualifying Pre-Packaged Vacation on a participating Tour Operator (Air Canada Vacations, Sunquest Vacations, Transat Holidays / Nolitours, and WestJet Vacations), and the price of your identical booking drops before you travel, the tour operator will honour the new lower price.

Each operator has certain conditions. Some tour operators charge an administration fee for processing a price drop request. This fee will either be deducted from the amount refunded, or processed by the tour operator as a separate charge.

Price Drop Protection is a year around program exclusive to FlightNetwork.com that allows you to lock in savings if the base price of your Flight, the total base price (before taxes) of your Hotel, or the total price (base + taxes & fees) of your Vacation package and the total base price (before taxes) of your Flight & Hotel Booking drops after you book.

If you've purchased a Flight at $500 (before taxes) and the price drops to $250 (before taxes), you will receive $250 Price Drop Protection Dollars to spend on any new Flight, Hotel, Vacation, Flight & Hotel, or Insurance booking. Your protection per person is unlimited, and you can grab a deal up until the time your flight departs.

If you are flying internationally and booked directly with an American airline, check out Yapta.com. This website tracks the flight prices after you book. The following airlines give you future airline credit depending on the price difference:

- Alaska

- American
- AirTran
- Delta
- Hawaiian
- JetBlue
- United
- US Airways
- Virgin America

Sales from your airport

Have you tried using Airfarewatchdog.com? This website finds the best fares and seat sales from airports. What I like about this is that it finds flights and destinations that you never thought of. I use this website in addition to travel aggregator websites, as it also includes discount carriers that are often not included on other search engines. All the deals are posted manually, and tested before being posted.

Bid for Travel

Compete4YourSeat.com is the only cost free service that allows travel professionals to bid for your business.

How this website works is that you create a sample itinerary and it gets sent to all the travel agents on the website. Each agent can then bid on the flight.

Once they make a bid, you receive an email and if you like the offer, you can contact the travel agent to make the sale. It's as simple as that, the consumer wins, the travel agent wins.

Avoid flying during high demand periods

Christmas seat sales on domestic flights in Canada do not exist. If you absolutely have to fly during this time (usually December 15 to January 8), you may as well just bite the bullet now.

Other high demand periods of the year include anything involving a long weekend, and school breaks.

Small business discounts

Have you heard of the Air Canada Rewards for Small Business Program?

Some of the benefits of this free membership include:

- One-time 15% flight booking discount
- Up to 10% discount on Maple Leaf Club memberships
- One-time complimentary Maple Leaf Lounge access
- Five (5) prepaid OnBoard Café vouchers

Free stopovers

Many travelers don't know much about stopovers. When flying across the world, most airlines have to stop somewhere en route to the final destination. Some airlines allow you to stopover in certain cities for a few days for no extra charge.

Here are some ideas for some international destinations:

Dubai

If flying Emirates Airlines, you may have a layover in Dubai. You can consult their website for special hotel packages. There is a maximum stay of 96 hours for passengers requiring visas.

Iceland

Icelandair makes it easy for travelers to stopover in Iceland on a flight to Europe. Icelandair offers customers the option of stopping over in Iceland at no extra charge. With most fares, a stopover in Iceland cannot exceed four nights, and must be in one direction only. Special hotel rates are available to passengers stopping over in Iceland en route to/from Europe.

Singapore

There are many ways to stop over in Singapore, whether you are heading to Europe from Australia, vice versa, or from the United States to various places throughout Southeast Asia and the South Pacific.

Singapore Air offers a Singapore Stopover Holiday package that includes:

- Accommodation for one night at a hotel in an applicable category
- 50% discount on the à la carte food menu, only at the designated food outlet at the passenger's hotel
- Transfers between airport and hotel on a seat-in-coach basis
- Free unlimited rides on SIA Hop-on Bus
- Free admission to key attractions & other complimentary deals

London, England

American Airlines and British Airlines both offer stopovers in London on certain routes. This would be possible if you're flying elsewhere in Europe, and in some cases, on the way to various places in Africa. Before booking online, make sure to check with the airline, as rules differ for every flight.

Istanbul

If you're flying on Turkish Airlines and switching flights, and you have a layover of six hours or more, you can head to the airport's Hotel Information Desk to partake in a free tour with a private guide. Stops on the tours usually include time at the Blue Mosque, Topkapi Palace, and the Grand Bazaar.

Cook Islands

If you are headed to New Zealand, you can get a free stopover in the Cook Islands when you book with Air New Zealand (a member of the Star Alliance). They permit a free stopover in the alluring Cook Islands in either direction when travelling via Los Angeles to or from Australia. You may also wish to make a stopover in Auckland at no extra charge.

Achieve Star Alliance Gold with Aegean Airlines

Have you ever heard of Aegean Airlines? Aegean Airlines is a regional airline based in Greece (large Greek airline), and is one of the members in the Star Alliance.

This airline has a frequent flyer program called Miles & Bonus. This program has low mileage requirements for Elite status, compared to other airlines in the Star Alliance.

You earn 1,000 miles just for registering, and you earn Star Alliance silver status after just 4,000 miles within a year (including the 1,000 for joining), and then need only 16,000 more within a year for Gold. Once you achieve their Gold status, you only need to fly once every thirty six months to maintain that status.

Star Alliance member Air Canada requires you to fly 25,000 Altitude Qualifying Miles (AQM) or 25 Altitude Qualifying Segments (AQS) for the equivalent Star Alliance Silver Status. To achieve Star Alliance Gold, they require you to fly 50,000 Altitude Qualifying Miles (AQM) or 50 Altitude Qualifying Segments (AQS).

Here are some of the benefits that you get when you have Star Alliance Silver Status and you fly with a partner on the Star Alliance:

- Priority Reservations Waitlisting - when there aren't any seats available on your preferred flight, the airline will ensure that you sit at the top of the waiting list for another.

- Priority Airport Standby - should your meeting overrun and you miss your flight, airline staff will arrange for you to be on the next available flight.

Here are some of the benefits that you get when you have Star Alliance Gold Status and you fly with a partner on the Star Alliance:

- Priority Airport Check-in - Star Alliance Gold Status allows you to check-in through the Priority check-in counters.

- Airport Lounge Access - You and a guest can escape the crowds and relax in over 1,000 airport lounges worldwide, regardless of your class of travel.

- Priority Boarding - Enjoy the freedom of boarding at your convenience, along with First and Business Class passengers.

- Extra Baggage Allowance –You are allowed an additional 20 kg (44 pounds) where the weight concept applies, or one additional piece of luggage where the piece concept applies.

- Priority Baggage Handling - Your bags get priority treatment, and are among the first to be unloaded.

If you fly with Air Canada and other Star Alliance partners, I recommend looking into joining the Aegean Miles and Bonus program because of the easier mileage qualifications requirements.

All-inclusive holidays

Many Canadians enjoy all-inclusive holidays, as they can be a good value. An all-inclusive package is the same as a regular flight and hotel package, except that all your meals, beverages, transportation to the resort from the airport, and alcoholic drinks are included in the price. Popular destinations include: Mexico, Cuba, the Dominican Republic, and Jamaica.

Some of the more popular on-line travel agents that specialize in these holidays include: RedTag, iTravel2000, Flight Centre, Signature Vacations, and Marlin Travel.

Some of these holidays may be a good deal if you have children under 12 years old (usually free), and/or enjoy a few drinks. Personally, I have been on a few of these holidays, and I recommend reading as many reviews about the resort as possible on independent review websites like TripAdvisor. These websites will allow travelers to post their own photos and comments about their stay.

Elite Status Matching

Did you know that if you are an Elite flyer on one airline that some companies will match Elite status with their loyalty program? For example, if you are an Elite passenger with Air Canada, Delta, or Alaska Airlines, you can request Elite or equivalent access with other airlines. Having Elite status is a great benefit as you earn free lounge access, upgrades, and no luggage fees.

Tools

- Kayak - http://www.kayak.com/

- Skyscanner - http://www.skyscanner.ca

- Momondo - http://www.momondo.com

- International Student Identity Card -

  http://www.isiccanada.ca/

- Travel CUTS - http://www.travelcuts.com/

- Air Canada Student Pass -

  http://www.canadiantravelhacking.com/go/ac-stu

- Sunwing - http://www.sunwing.ca/

- Flightfox -

  http://www.canadiantravelhacking.com/go/flightfox

- Great Canadian Rebates -

  http://www.canadiantravelhacking.com/go/gcr

- Ebates -

  http://www.canadiantravelhacking.com/go/ebates

- AlternateAirports.com -

  http://www.alternateairports.com

- FlightNetwork.com - http://www.flightnetwork.com

- Yapta - http://www.yapta.com

- Airfarewatchdog - http://www.airfarewatchdog.com

- Compete4YourSeat - http://www.compete4yourseat.com

- Air Canada Rewards for Small Business Program - http://www.canadiantravelhacking.com/go/ac-biz

- Aegean Airlines - http://en.aegeanair.com/

- RedTag - http://www.redtag.ca

- iTravel2000 - http://www.itravel2000.com

- Flight Centre - http://www.flightcentre.ca/

- Signature Vacations -

  http://www.signaturevacations.com/

- Marlin Travel - http://www.marlintravel.ca/

- TripAdvisor – http://www.tripadvisor.ca

Section 2: Accommodation

Chapter 5

Priceline® / Hotwire® Strategies

Priceline®

I enjoy staying in nice hotels but I hate paying full price for them! I have been using this website for years. Priceline.com lets you bid for a hotel room. Priceline® has access to the excess hotel room inventory that hotel chains have. These are rooms that they believe they will not be able to book for a certain date. Priceline® is able to acquire these rooms at a low price, and allow you to bid on this inventory.

This type of booking is called opaque, because you will not see which hotel you are staying at until the purchase is confirmed.

I have some great tips in this chapter that will help you get the rock-bottom price for your room. Before I explain some of my Priceline® bidding tips, I wanted to show how the Priceline.com works.

There are three main ways to book a hotel room on Priceline®:

1. List View

The results of your city search criteria are shown on this view. You can see the name of the hotel, and the exact price is displayed. You are able to sort by hotel name, distance from city center, price, and overall popularity.

Priceline List view.

2. Express Deals

The hotels listed on this tab show the price of the hotel, location, ratings, and amenities, such as a pool, restaurant, fitness center, or free Internet. You will not see the name or precise location of the property.

Priceline Express Deals view.

I have discovered that often you can figure out the identity of the hotel by the description and amenities listed. For example, this listing lets you choose your bed type, and based on the specific names of the room, the hotel is likely to be the Delta Vancouver.

Sample Priceline Express Deal.

If you book a Priceline® Express Deal and find a cheaper rate for this hotel, any time until the day before check-in, Priceline will match that price and give you an additional $25, with some conditions, of course.

There is no bidding involved using Express Deals, so it lets you find the location and amenities you need. If you are not comfortable bidding on a hotel room, I suggest using this alternative, to save some money over the standard room rate.

3. Name Your Own Price®

This option lets you bid on a hotel room. This option can potentially save you the most on your hotel room. Two main caveats: reservations are almost never refundable, and you do not have choice in the hotel amenities (hotel may not have a pool or restaurant). Additionally, the bids are always for two adults (so you may get stuck with a king-size bed for three adults). I always make sure that if I used the Name Your Own Price option that my travel dates will not change. Do not use Name Your Own Price if you only prefer to stay at Hilton brand hotels, or if your room must have a coffee maker.

When you bid on a hotel on Priceline®, the website will ask you specifically where you want to stay inside the city based on zones.

Here is a sample example of the available zones in Vancouver, British Columbia.

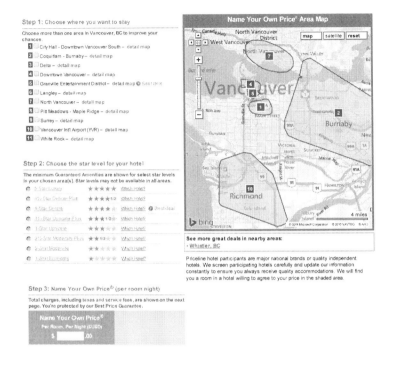

Priceline® Bidding Map.

Look carefully at the map, and understand each zone, and how close you need to be to the airport or city center. Staying outside the city may or may not be worth it to you.

Clicking on the detail map hyperlink next to each zone will show a larger view of the area.

Priceline® Name Your Own Price® Area Map

You can choose one zone or multiple zones where you would like to stay. As soon as at least one zone is selected, you can choose which star level of hotel you would like to bid for. When you choose a star level, you are bidding on every hotel at that level and above. If you select a zone, sometimes you will notice that not all star levels are available to be chosen. This means the zone does not have any star levels in that zone to bid in.

Step 1: Choose where you want to stay

Choose more than one area in Vancouver, BC to improve your chances.

1. City Hall - Downtown Vancouver South – detail map
2. Coquitlam - Burnaby – detail map
3. Delta – detail map
4. Downtown Vancouver – detail map
5. Granville Entertainment District – detail map
6. ✓ Langley – detail map
7. North Vancouver – detail map
8. Pitt Meadows - Maple Ridge – detail map
9. Surrey – detail map
10. Vancouver Intl Airport (YVR) – detail map
11. White Rock – detail map

Step 2: Choose the star level for your hotel

The minimum Guaranteed Amenities are shown for select star levels in your chosen area(s). Star levels may not be available in all areas.

5-Star Luxury	★★★★★	Which Hotel?
4½-Star Deluxe-Plus	★★★★½	Which Hotel?
4-Star Deluxe	★★★★	Which Hotel?
3½-Star Upscale-Plus	★★★½	Which Hotel?
3-Star Upscale	★★★	Which Hotel?
2½-Star Moderate-Plus	★★½	Which Hotel?
2-Star Moderate	★★	Which Hotel?
1-Star Economy	★	Which Hotel?

No hotels available above 3.5 stars in Langley, BC on Priceline bidding.

One of the first questions most people ask when they start to use the Name Your Own Price® option on Priceline® is, what should I start the bidding at?

My experience tells me that I need to see what general prices for hotels are available elsewhere on other websites. I look first at the Express Deals option to see what is available to purchase as opposed to bidding. If the city is full for a sporting event or convention, expect prices to be higher.

I go on Hotels.com to see what the four-star hotels are selling for, and it will sometimes tell me how many rooms are left at certain hotels so that I can see the demand. If many hotels are not available on Hotels.com, this tells me that availability is low, and that I should have a higher starting bid.

Another resource is The Bidding Traveller. This website lets you see the past successful bids for the city you are bidding on. It lets you see what hotels were available at a certain star level, and the price range of successful bids. This is a nice resource to have, as it lets you know the successful bid history for that city for Priceline. It also gives you an expectation of the hotels available for a certain star level in a city, based on past bids.

Another forum that shows past Priceline® successful bids is Betterbidding.com. They have each major city broken down by thread, and help give you a feel of what price you should be bidding.

Typically, if Priceline® does not accept your offer, you can change the star level or area you requested, and try again immediately. Or, you can try your exact same request again 24 hours later.

If you had a successful bid, your hotel will be shown immediately after purchase. Your hotel will be from either a national hotel chain or a preferred independent hotel partner.

Remember, that   hotels are non-refundable, non-transferable, and non-changeable even if the reservation is not used.

Bidding Strategy

Even though I am getting a discount for my hotel stay because I do not know what the hotel name, I want to make sure that I maximize my discount.

Before you start to bid for a room, it is best to first do some research. Find out the current retail prices using other websites before you start to bid.

I always start my bid at 40-50% off the lowest Express Deal in the zone where I am looking to stay. As an example, if the Express Deal for a four-star hotel in Downtown Vancouver is $101 per night, I would start my bid at around $60-65, depending on my urgency to get a room reservation. The maximum I recommend bidding is $10 less than the same star rating in the zone that I am bidding on. In this case, I would bid up to $90 per night.

Free re-bids

I have a trick that will get you a free-rebid. Remember, earlier in the chapter, where I showed that not all star levels are available to be chosen in a zone? If you wanted to stay at a four-star hotel in Zone 4 (Downtown Vancouver) and the first bid was rejected, simply increase your bid and add a zone that doesn't have a four-star hotel in its zone. You can continue this pattern of bidding until you have an accepted bid or you run out of re-bids. If you run out of free re-bids, just wait 24 hours.

Priceline® Change Requests

On one of our first trips together to Hawaii, my wife and I booked a hotel on the island of Oahu, when we were going to the Big Island. We called Priceline® to get this exception, but we had to rebid again for the right dates and location. You will typically only receive a refund if you win another bid. We still had to pay a service charge for cancelling the reservation (around $30 Canadian), but it saved us hundreds.

Use a cash back website like Ebates

If you use a cash back website, you will receive up to 5% cash back when you book any Priceline Name Your Own Price Hotel using Ebates.

Ebates for Priceline purchases.

Purchases you make at Ebates stores are credited if you start your shopping session at Ebates.com, and click to a store via an Ebates link.

Triple-check your bid

Triple check your dates. The date selectors on the Priceline® home page tend to get a little bit slippery, and it's easy to choose the wrong month. Check the month and day on every page, over and over again. You may be booking the right date in the wrong month.

Priceline® tips

Here are some tips before you start bidding on Priceline®:

- If you stay at a resort in Priceline®, expect to pay resort fees, which can be around $10-20 per day per person. These fees are not a part of your winning bid.

- When looking at the map for a city, pay extra attention to the zones. In Miami, the South beach zone has hotels that can be a considerable distance from the actual South Beach. In Las Vegas, the Las Vegas Strip Vicinity North zone has hotels that can be off the main strip by a fair distance.

- Parking is also extra, so be aware that you could pay up to $20 per night, as this fee is not included as part of your winning bid.

- Taxes are also not seen until the payment page, and this could be significant in some cities (tourism tax, hotel tax, and general state or provincial taxes).

- Priceline® bids are non-refundable, and you must input your credit card information before making a bid. Make sure that you double-check your zones, desired star-rating, and final price on the confirmation page.

- If you get a successful bid, place a call to the hotel to confirm your reservation with the type of room and/or bed you want.

- Try not to bid below a four-star hotel. I find that the best deals are for four-star hotels and higher. Also, the quality of the hotel can be questionable at the lower star-levels. Some hotels that Priceline considers three and a half star, I consider a three or lower.

Hotwire®

When 3-star and 4-star hotels have unsold rooms, they use Hotwire to fill them, so you get them at prices lower than booking directly at the hotel. Hotwire® is similar to Priceline®, where you are shown the name of the hotel after you book to get hotel stays that are significantly below published prices.

When you visit Hotwire.com, you simply choose the Hotels option and enter your destination, dates, number of rooms, and number of adults and children that are staying.

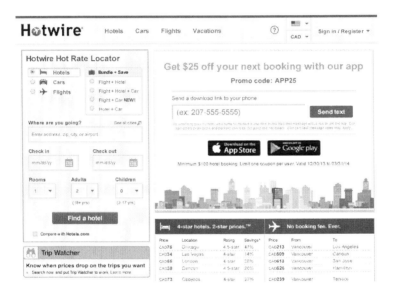

Hotwire® Hotel Search.

After pressing the Find a hotel button, Hotwire® will take you to a page where you will see two tabs, Hotwire® Hot Rates and Standard Rates. The Standard Rates tab just shows hotels and the price per night is next to each listing. The Hotwire® Hot Rates tab breaks down the city by zone and star-rating.

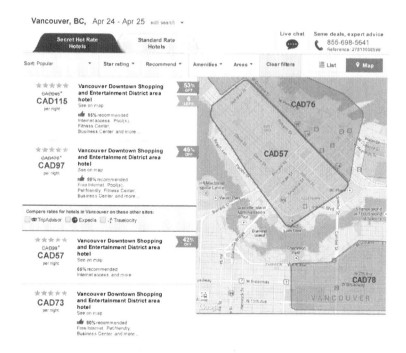

A Hotwire® Hot Rates zone and description.

In each zone you will see that price per room and included amenities are shown. If you click on the Area Map hyperlink, you will see what the zone boundaries are for the map.

Hotwire Map for Vancouver, BC.

Another nice feature in Hotwire® is that they provide a small sample of the hotels in that particular zone at the star-rating you are looking at. My experience has been that I rarely get a hotel that appears in this list, but that gives me enough information to make an educated guess as to which hotel I might get.

On the side of the page, you will find additional filters like star-rating, reviews, price, and hotel amenities. This is a nice feature, because if you are looking for a hotel with an indoor pool or free breakfast or free Internet, you can filter out hotels where those amenities are not available.

How to get a good price on Hotwire®?

Before you start to look closely at the prices, I recommend looking at historical information on what other users have received for hotel prices using Hotwire®.

I recommend using the website Hotels Deals Revealed. This is a forum where former Hotwire® users name the hotels they received from Hotwire®. Each user shares the price that they paid, along with the star rating, dates, and amenities included.

Another great resource is Better Bidding. This is another forum website where locations are organized by geographical area. The list in each thread list is only a compilation of hotels that have already been reported on the forum.

How to guess which hotel you'll get on Hotwire®

One of the main reasons people avoid using Hotwire is the uncertainty in the hotel they are getting for a successful bid. I wanted to show an example of how you can use a combination of the Trip Advisor rating, amenities list, and other tools to make an educated guess to see what hotel is being offered to you.

We will work this sample listing in Orlando, Florida. It is rated a four-star hotel in the SeaWorld South area with a Fitness Center, Pool(s), Business Center, and Laundry Facilities (self-service).

Hotwire® Hot Rates.

If you click the "Book now" red box you will learn more details about the actual hotel. If you scroll down near the bottom of the page, you will see the customer ratings courtesy of TripAdvisor.com.

TripAdvisor information about Hotwire listing.

This shows that the mystery hotel has an average rating of 3.5 out of 5 on the TripAdvisor® website. Take a close look at the TripAdvisor® results and narrow down the star-level, and try to match the amenities and TripAdvisor® rating.

If you are unsuccessful matching up the mystery hotel, try using the website Hotwire® Revealed. Their results page will list all of the current Hotwire.com deals that match your criteria. Once you've found a hotel description you like, click the Reveal button to see which hotels it's likely to be. The higher the match percentage of a particular hotel, the better the match between that hotel and the description you've selected.

Here is a sample of a reveal from Hotwire® Revealed.

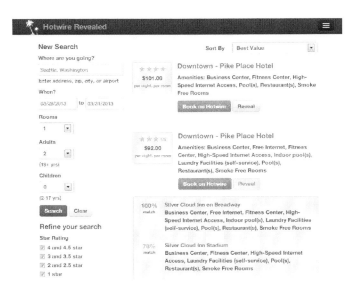

Sample Reveal on Hotwire Revealed.

The final recommendation I have is to use the Bid Goggles website. This website is a sophisticated database of Hotwire hotels. Bid Googles uses information sent to them from other Hotwire users that have recently made a purchase. The website matches the Hotwire description with the description of similar hotels that other travelers have visited.

Here is an example of a hotel search in Victoria, BC. One of the listings is for a four-star hotel for $94 per night. When I hover over the **See hotels in this class** hyperlink, the popup brings up hotels like the Victoria Marriott Inner Harbour, Delta Victoria Ocean Pointe, and the Fairmont Empress. The amenities for this hotel are also shown in the listing at the bottom.

Sample Hotwire listing.

With the information that you have from Hotwire®, copy the hotel's amenities, star rating, and location into the Bid Goggles website and the tool will attempt to match that mystery hotel to a hotel in its database.

Bid Googles Search.

Reasons why you shouldn't use Hotwire®

Hotwire® can save you money on your hotel room, but read these tips before you start booking:

1. Your booking is non-refundable.

All sales are final on Hotwire.com. I always wait until I am sure I will be making the reservation and not making any changes. I recommend booking a hotel that offers a free cancellation policy prior to booking with Hotwire®. This gives you a backup plan.

2. You will not earn points for your hotel's loyalty program.

When staying using Hotwire® bookings, you will not earn any loyalty points. This means no points for the stay, and none of the benefits you might have by being a loyalty program member. If you have status in a hotel loyalty program, and want to take advantage of the benefits of that, you shouldn't use Hotwire as your booking engine.

3. Hotels have the option to give you status benefits.

As a status member with several hotel chains including, Hilton, Marriott, and Priority Club, I have come to expect free Internet, lounge, and some type of breakfast. Booking through websites like Expedia or Hotwire, it is up to the hotel to decide if I am still eligible to receive these benefits.

4. Resort fees and parking are not included in the price.

These fees can be close to $20 per day, so they can certainly add up.

Chapter 6

Hotel Hacks

Have you ever noticed that most major hotel chain websites or online travel agents like Expedia® and Priceline® guarantee that they have the lowest prices on their websites compared to the competition? This makes the decision easy for most people, thinking that if a major website can offer a guarantee like that, their prices must be the lowest.

If you find a lower price for the same reservation, most websites will not just match the lower rate, but provide additional discounts, bonus points, other benefits, or even free nights!

This chapter will show you how you can guarantee yourself the lowest price with each major travel website and hotel chains.

Expedia® Best Rate Guarantee

The Expedia® Best Price Guarantee says that if you find a better price for the exact same hotel room within 24 hours of booking a room on Expedia®, and fill in an online form, they will match the price by refunding back to your credit card the difference, and deposit a $50 voucher in your Expedia® account for a future booking.

Expedia® Rewards members, also qualify for an extended Hotel Price Guarantee that provides price matching up until 24 hours before your hotel stay.

Expedia Best Price Guarantee.

Here is how to check if the current Expedia® hotel booking you have is the lowest price:

1. Use an aggregator website like Hotelscombined.com or Kayak.com to see the rates for the hotel for multiple websites. I like these websites, because they have a built in currency tool (lets you compare apples to apples). This lets you comparison shop quite easily. Kayak.com highlights the price range within each listing.

This is a sample Kayak.com listing.

2. You can fill out an online form and wait for a response over e-mail. This can take as short as ten minutes to as long as several hours to get the claim approved and processed.

It can take up to several days to see your $50 voucher in your Expedia® account, but it is usually quick. You must pay for your room with Expedia upfront to file a claim. It can be a refundable or non-refundable reservation. I always do prepaid but refundable reservations.

Keep in mind that the claim must be filed within 24 hours of booking the room, and the room must be an exact match between the competing websites.

The maximum number of travel coupons that you can earn in one month is three. You can only use one voucher per reservation, and they do not expire for one year.

Choice Hotels

The Choice Hotels chain also promises to have the lowest prices for its properties with its Best Internet Rate Guarantee policy:

- Comfort Inn
- Comfort Suites
- Quality Inn
- Sleep Inn
- Clarion
- Cambria Suites
- MainStay Suites
- Suburban
- Econo Lodge
- Rodeway Inn

If you find a lower rate, you need to contact Choice hotels via an online form.

Hilton Best Rate Guarantee

Hilton promises that if you find a lower rate through any other booking channel, they will match that rate you found plus, for hotels in the U.S.A., Puerto Rico, Canada or Mexico, they will give you a $50 American Express Gift Cheque. For hotels outside the U.S., Puerto Rico, Canada or Mexico, they will take U.S. $50 off of your bill.

Just book through any Hilton Family website, reservation center or hotel directly.

In fact, we promise that if you find a lower rate through any other booking channel, we'll match that rate you found plus:

> For hotels in the U.S.A., Puerto Rico, Canada or Mexico, we'll give you a $50 American Express® Gift Cheque. Terms and Conditions.

> For hotels outside the U.S., Puerto Rico, Canada or Mexico, we'll take US $50 off of your bill. Terms and Conditions.

No matter where your destination is, if you have found a better rate through another booking channel, submit a claim and our Guest Assistance team will determine eligibility and contact you.

Hilton Best Rates

You must have a confirmed reservation made through one of the following official Hilton Worldwide booking channels:

- Any official Hilton Worldwide website
- Hilton Reservations & Customer Care
- Directly at a hotel in the Hilton Worldwide portfolio
- Through an IATA accredited retail travel agent professional ("Travel Agent") booking through a Hilton Worldwide channel or the following Global Distribution Systems: Amadeus, Apollo/Galileo, Worldspan, and SABRE.

You must find a **lower publicly available rate** on a non-Hilton Worldwide booking channel (except for opaque websites like Priceline or Hotwire) for the same accommodations. "Same Accommodations" means the same room type, at the same hotel, with the same dates and length of stay, same number of guests, same designation as either cancellable or non-cancellable, same advance purchase policies, and the same terms and conditions governing the room rate.

You must submit your claim within 24 hours of making your reservation, and at least 24 hours prior to your arrival at the hotel.

You may only submit one claim for each stay. A **stay** means the total number of consecutive nights spent at the same hotel by the same guest or guests.

You can submit a claim via an online form or via their toll-free phone number.

Hyatt

Hyatt offers its Best Rate Guarantee when you book on Hyatt.com. With no booking fees, you can book any Hyatt brand including Park Hyatt, Andaz, Grand Hyatt, Hyatt Regency, Hyatt Place, and Hyatt Summerfield Suites.

If you find a lower, published rate on another site, they will not just match the rate, they will discount it by 20% for your entire stay.

This program lets you claim over the phone prior to booking with Hyatt. The representative will be able to verify the rate immediately without any delay. The rate must be for the same hotel, type of accommodations, room type, and bed type, as well as the same dates and number of guests.

InterContinental Hotels Group Best Price Guarantee

The Best Price Guarantee is the lowest price guarantee promising the best hotel room prices for any InterContinental Hotels Group (IHG) property.

Hotel properties include:

- InterContinental Hotels & Resorts
- Crowne Plaza Hotels & Resorts
- Holiday Inn Hotels & Resorts
- Holiday Inn Express Hotels
- Hotel Indigo Hotels
- Staybridge Suites Hotels
- Candlewood Suites Hotels

If you find a lower room price (room rate) with a lower total room cost (including all taxes and fees) on a publicly available competing Web site for the same hotel, type of accommodations and rate restrictions on the same date(s), they will not only match that lower room price, they will give you your first night's room price free.

Make sure you use "Best Available" as your rate preference for the IHG hotel search.

IHG Rate Preference.

Here is a sample example of how a successful resolution works. You book a two night stay at the lowest available price through the Best Available Rate search for a hotel in Toronto, Ontario at a Holiday Inn or another IHG site for a room price of $200.00. Within 24 hours, you find a room price of $190.00 and the total room cost that is less than the total room cost for the IHG hotel on a competing Web site for the same hotel, same night, with the same rate restrictions (refundable or non-refundable), and same room type (same number and type of bed(s)).

You would contact IHG to claim the Best Price Guarantee, by filling out the online form. Once the Guest Relations team confirms that the Best Price Guarantee claim filed is valid, they will modify your reservation with the first night free and the second night at $190.00. If you had originally booked just a one night stay, your entire trip would be free!

Here is an example of a recent success I had with this program, where I scored a free hotel night, saving me over three hundred dollars.

Dear **Steven Zussino**,

Thank you for contacting IHG's Best Price Guarantee Support Desk in regards to your reservation at **Crowne Plaza Redondo Beach, CA** on **24 May 2013** for **1 night** under confirmation

We were able to verify the lower rate found on www.hotels.com and are pleased to award you a **FREE NIGHT** for **24 May 2013** at **Crowne Plaza Redondo Beach, CA.** This is not subject to additional adjustments. Please be informed that the Free Night is subject to the hotel's regular cancellation policy. Please contact the hotel directly to verify the cancellation policy of this booking.

Please also be reminded that once a valid claim has been made and approved by IHG for a specific date, no further claims by the same person will be accepted for the same date. If members of the same household make claims for consecutive nights at the same IHG hotel or at different IHG hotels within fifty (50) miles of each other, only the Best Price Guarantee claim for the first night will be honored. In the event of a valid claim, reservations are non-transferable after the claim is found to be valid, and the name on the reservation must remain the same as when the claim is verified and no additional names may be added to the reservation after the claim is found to be valid. Valid government issued ID is required upon check-in that matches the name found on the reservation.

We look forward to accommodating your upcoming reservation. Should you have any questions or concerns please contact us via e-mail at bestpriceguarantee@ihg.com or phone at 800.447.2981.

Best Internet Rate Guarantee Success.

Kimpton's Best Rate Guarantee

If you find a bookable rate online for any Kimpton hotel that is lower than what you will find on their own website, they will not only match the lower rate you found elsewhere, but they will provide a $25 food and beverage credit per stay.

Instead of an online form, this hotel lets you call them toll-free, and they can match prior to booking.

The rate must be available on the third-party website at the time of booking, and does not apply to rates found on bid-based websites such as Priceline.com and Hotwire.com.

Marriott Look No Further Rate guarantee

The Marriott hotel chain offers a low price guarantee on its properties called the Look No Further® (LNF) rate guarantee. If within 24 hours you find a lower rate elsewhere for the same room you've booked directly with Marriott, they will adjust your rate to be 25% less than the lower one. For example, if you reserved a room with Marriott for $100 and found a lower rate for $80, if your claim was validated, your new rate would be $60.

Look No Further Best Rate Guarantee

This is one of the better guarantees, as this lower rate and discount applies to the entire stay, plus you earn valuable reward miles for booking with the hotel chain directly.

Remember that to get a valid Look No Further® Best Rate, you will need to find a publicly available rate. This means that when you book your Marriott you do not use any CAA, senior, government, or corporate rates. These are examples of rates that are not publicly available rates, and do not qualify for LNF Best Rate Guarantee claims.

I recommend using the meta-search engines in the Tools area of this chapter to look for cheaper rates elsewhere.

Starwood®

If you find a lower rate prior to, or within 24 hours of, booking your hotel room at Starwood® Hotels, you can submit a Best Rate Guarantee Claim, and they will honor that lower rate. Not only will they lower the rate, but you get a choice of having the rate lowered by 10% or 2,000 Starpoints®. Based on the high value of Starpoints®, I recommend the Starpoints® option. A weekend night at a Category 1 hotel is just 2,000 Starpoints®.

What is like about this low rate guarantee program is that you do not need to make a prior reservation on another website for Starwood to match or beat the rate.

Why your claim will not be approved

Here are some of the main reasons why your claim with any of these programs will not be approved:

1. Most third-party websites are based on double occupancy.

    If you are attempting a claim with more than two adults in a room, it is challenging to find a reliable price. The hotel usually charges an extra person fee (can be $20 per night) but the third-party websites like Booking.com, simply show the price for the room based on double occupancy.

2. Verify the competitive rate, and that the room is available.

    Some websites will show availability on the search page, but when you actually try to book the room, the website displays a message that the "room is not available." Make sure that the hotel actually has availability with that booking website.

3. Match up the room types.

    If IHG labels a room, "2 QUEEN BEDS EXEC CLUB LEVEL," the other competing website's room type should be identical or have a similar description. I have seen other websites offer free parking or a breakfast package and, even though the competing website is cheaper, the rate will not qualify.

Four Seasons Preferred Partner Program

The Four Seasons Preferred Partner Program is an exclusive, invitation-only network of high-end travel consultants from around the world. These travel consultants provide their clients with a premium level of service, and share in the Four Seasons commitment to exceptional quality.

The Four Seasons Preferred Partner Program is an easy way to get extra benefits included when you stay at a Four Seasons Property.

These benefits have been standardized across all properties (from Las Vegas to Whistler):

- Daily full American breakfast for two people per bedroom, served through In-Room Dining or in the hotel restaurant (including buffets).

- Extra value-added amenity, such as: spa credit of $100 USD once during stay (not applicable to products); golf credit of $100 USD once during stay (not applicable to pro shop purchases); or lunch for two once during stay (up to $85 USD, excluding gratuity and alcohol). Each hotel's specific extra amenity is specified by the individual property.

- Upgrade of one category, based on availability at time of check-in (excluding signature suites and villas).

- Welcome note at check-in.

- Complimentary high-speed Internet access for all suite bookings.

These benefits are added at no additional cost.

Virtuoso® travel consultants

Virtuoso® is the industry's leading luxury travel network. This by-invitation-only organization comprises over 330 agencies with more than 7,200 elite travel advisors in 20 countries in North and South America, the Caribbean, Australia, and New Zealand, as well as over 1,300 of the world's best travel providers and premier destinations.

As a result of their membership in Virtuoso®, independent travel agencies receive sales, marketing and technology support, specialized training and accreditation programs, as well as exclusive services and products. Being a client of a Virtuoso® travel advisor means your travels will be customized to your specific desires by a foremost expert, and that you'll be recognized as one of the most prestigious guests in the world with all the privileged access, perks and service that implies.

Booking with a Virtuoso® travel advisor gets you access to some extra benefits and special rates:

- Early check in and late check out.
- $100 USD value in amenities credit (could be used for spa or food and beverages).
- Free breakfast for 2 guests.
- Complimentary upgrade at the time of booking or if available upon arrival.
- Voyager Club - exclusive cruise rewards.
- Preferred pricing.
- Complimentary full day or evening excursions.
- Cocktail reception.

Using the certified Virtuoso® travel advisor website you will see all the available rates of each Virtuoso® hotel.

Virtuoso Rates.

In this example, the best available rate at the Four Seasons Whistler is the same as the Virtuoso® rate but the Virtuoso® rate includes extra benefits like:

- Upgrade to the next room type at time of check in (subject to availability)

- Chef's choice welcome amenity

- Continental breakfast or any items of equal or lesser value up to $48.00 for two persons per room for each morning through in room dining or the restaurant, excluding gratuity.

- In room dining valued at $85.00 once during stay excluding gratuity and alcohol.

Corporate or Membership Rate discount

Using a corporate rate for your hotel booking is a great way to get a discount. Larger companies or governments negotiate discounted rates with hotel chains, and allow their employees to use the discount rate for both personal and business travel.

If you are a teacher, professional, union member, or member of a Chamber of Commerce, etc., check to see if any discounts are available.

Here is an example of a professional organization, the Canadian Bar Association, providing a 10% discount off the best available rate of the day at Starwood hotels to its members.

Canadian Bar Association Starwood Hotels Discount.

To find out if your company or alumni association has a corporate discount, contact your company's travel services, human resources or finance department. In some cases, companies arrange a special corporate rate with a particular hotel. Therefore, you may need to call the hotel directly to make reservations.

Each chain has different rules and rates.

Marriott has a special Canadian Federal Government rate for all Federal government employees in Canada and provincial government employees of the following five Canadian provinces and territories: Alberta, New Brunswick, Ontario, Yukon Territory, and Northwest Territories.

CAA Discounts

Having a CAA membership not only gives you great peace of mind when driving but you also get nice discounts at hotels.

Did you know that you are entitled to these discounts?

Accent Inns

- Save 5% off advertised promotional rates, which may include special packages and internet specials.

Best Western

- Save 10% or more on best available room rates
- Children under 12 stay free with accompanying adult.
- Earn CAA Dollars

Hilton

- Save up to 5% off the Best Available Rate in the US and Canada, subject to availability and may not apply to all room types
- Children under 18 stay free with accompanying adult

Hyatt

- Receive a 10% discount for requested room type at time of booking

Marriott

- Save a minimum of 5% off standard rates based on room availability

Starwood

- Save 5-15% at any participating Starwood Hotels & Resorts with 14 days advance purchase
- Receive complimentary Preferred Plus status in Starwood's Preferred Guest® program, which includes: (Instant upgrade to a preferred room at check-in; 4 p.m. late checkout; Two Starpoints® for every dollar spent).

AARP® Discounts

AARP® is a non-profit, nonpartisan organization that helps people 50 and older improve the quality of their lives.

A membership for Canadians is just $17.00 U.S. for a one-year term.

Members receive up to 20% off hotels and resorts like Best Western, Choice, Hilton, Hyatt Hotels and Resorts®, LaQuinta Inns & Suites, MGM Resorts International™, Starwood Hotels and Resorts and Wyndham Worldwide.

At some of the hotel chains like Starwood Hotels you do not even need to have an AARP membership; you just need to be a senior (over 50 years old). If you are booking for a hotel with more than one adult, as long as one adult meets the senior qualification, the rate discount applies. On a recent trip to Bellevue, Washington, taken with my mother and family, we received the AARP rate and saved over $60 a night.

Tools

- HotelsCombined - http://www.canadiantravelhacking.com/go/h-c/

- Kayak – http://www.kayak.com

- Trivago.com – http://www.trivago.com

- Wego.com – http://www.wego.com

- Expedia - http://www.canadiantravelhacking.com/go/expedia-g

- Choice – http://www.canadiantravelhacking.com/go/choice-g

- Hyatt - http://www.canadiantravelhacking.com/go/hyatt-g

- InterContinental Hotels Group Best Price Guarantee - http://www.canadiantravelhacking.com/go/ihg-g

- Hilton's Best Rate Guarantee -
http://www.canadiantravelhacking.com/go/hilton-g

- Kimpton's Best Rate Guarantee -
http://www.canadiantravelhacking.com/go/kimpton-g

- Marriott - http://www.canadiantravelhacking.com/go/marriott-g

- Starwood - http://www.canadiantravelhacking.com/go/starwood-g

- Four Seasons Preferred Partner – http://www.canadiantravelhacking.com/go/4-s-pp

- AARP – http://www.aarp.org

- Virtuoso - http://www.virtuoso.com/

- CAA - http://www.caa.ca

Chapter 7

Hotel Loyalty Programs

Almost all of major hotel chains have a loyalty program. Since joining hotel loyalty programs is free, I always recommend registering. This chapter will review the major loyalty programs, and share some of the benefits that being a member provides.

In the Tools area at the back of the chapter, I have included links to sign up for each loyalty program.

Coast Hotels

Coast Hotels is a hotel chain in western North America with over 40 hotels and resorts in the states of Alaska, Arizona, Hawaii, Washington, Oregon, California, Idaho, and in the Canadian provinces of British Columbia, Alberta, and the Northwest Territories. Every pre-tax dollar that you spend towards applicable rates or packages at Coast Hotels & Resorts, including room and dining charges, earns Coast Rewards points.

Coast Hotels

This program lets you choose between collecting Coast Rewards points, Alaska Airline Miles or Aeroplan® Miles. You can earn up to 500 miles per stay with either Aeroplan® or Alaska Airmiles.

Coast Hotels and Resorts range from suburban and airport properties such as those in Greater Vancouver; Edmonton, Alberta; Calgary, Alberta; Seattle, Washington and Portland, Oregon to resort-designated properties such as: The Coast Osoyoos Beach Hotel in Osoyoos, British Columbia; The Coast Sundance Lodge in Sun Peaks, British Columbia; The Coast Pyramid Lake (Alberta) Resort in Jasper, Alberta; the Hillcrest Hotel, a Coast Resort in Revelstoke, British Columbia; the Maui Coast Hotel in Maui, Hawaii, and the Coast Capri Hotel, in Kelowna, British Columbia.

Fairmont President's Club

Fairmont Hotels & Resorts is a Canadian-based operator of luxury hotels and resorts.

Fairmont President's Club

Currently, Fairmont operates properties in 19 countries including Canada, the United States, Azerbaijan, Barbados, Bermuda, People's Republic of China, Egypt, Germany, India, Kenya, Kiev, Mexico, Monaco, the Philippines, Saudi Arabia, Singapore, South Africa, Switzerland, Ukraine, the United Arab Emirates, and United Kingdom.

Fairmont is known in Canada for its famous historic hotels and resorts such as the Empress Hotel (Victoria) and Hotel Vancouver in British Columbia, the Palliser in Calgary, the Château Laurier in Ottawa, the Royal York in Toronto, Banff Springs in Alberta, and Château Frontenac in Quebec City.

The Fairmont Banff Springs Hotel

Many of these hotels were originally built by the Canadian Pacific Railway in the late 19th and early 20th centuries.

The Fairmont President's Club is the Fairmont loyalty program. This program has three tiers: Club, Premier, and Platinum.

1. Club

This is the base level of the President's Club membership. Fairmont President's Club members are eligible for 500 base miles on qualifying stays from January 1- December 31.

2. Premier

Club Premier membership is awarded to members with either five stays or 10 room nights during a calendar year (January 1 – December 31). For each qualifying stay between January 1 and December 31, Premier members earn 250 bonus miles per qualifying stay (in addition to the regular 500 miles).

3. Platinum

Club Platinum membership is awarded to members with either 10 stays or 30 room nights during a calendar year (January 1 – December 31). Platinum members earn 500 bonus miles per qualifying stay (in addition to the regular 500 miles).

Members must re-qualify each year for the following year's membership. The membership year runs from March 1st through until February 28th.

Fairmont considers a qualifying stay as one that is booked under one of the following rates: published rack, package, and corporate. Examples of non-eligible stays are discounted rates (CAA, AARP), meetings, conventions, groups, and government rates.

All members receive these benefits:

- Complimentary, in-room high-speed Internet access
- Complimentary local calls and no service charge on toll-free calls
- Complimentary health club access (excluding spas)
- Complimentary shoeshine (city-center hotels)
- Daily room delivery of local or national newspaper
- 10% savings on Willow Stream Spa treatments and products
- 15% savings at The Fairmont Store
- Great Rates - Great Dates (exclusive savings on Fairmont getaways)
- Two-for-one rounds of golf at select Fairmont golf resorts
- Complimentary use of TaylorMade® golf clubs at select hotels
- Fairmont Fit (in-room delivery of Reebok shoes and apparel, yoga mats, stretch bands, and use of MP3 player)
- Complimentary access to BMW bikes at select hotels and resorts

Kimpton Hotels

Kimpton Hotels is a boutique hotel chain with hotels around the United States.

Kimpton Hotels

They have a loyalty program that rewards you based on nights stayed or number of stays, not points acquired like other programs. It has two levels, InTouch and Inner Circle, which reward you for staying at Kimpton hotels.

As an InTouch member, you get to enjoy these benefits:

- Exclusive offers all year long.
- You can **Raid the Mini Bar** in your guest room at every stay, up to $10.
- Free WiFi in your guest room, and throughout the hotel.
- Free nights earned by making a reservation directly.
- Invitations to InTouch parties and dinners in select cities.

There are two ways to earn complimentary night rewards. You will either receive a free night after 7 eligible stays or 20 eligible nights at Kimpton hotels, whichever comes first.

An eligible stay is one that is booked on their corporate website or over the phone with the InTouch Service Desk.

To help you understand, here are two scenarios.

Let's say you travel to Washington, D.C. for business every month, staying two nights on average each time. You'll receive a free night after your 7th trip.

The Inner Circle members are true VIPs. In addition to their InTouch benefits, they enjoy perks like:

- A favorite snack waiting for you.
- A complimentary room upgrade at check-in (when available).
- A complimentary chef's treat at their restaurants.
- A free night at their new hotels.
- An exclusive VIP reservation line.
- Direct access to the CEO via email.

If you're traveling to a lot of places, you could earn a Passport Reward. Just stay at 10 or more different Kimpton hotels during the calendar year (January 1 - December 31), and you'll receive an additional two-night complimentary stay.

Hotels.com Welcome Rewards program

With Hotels.com's Welcome Rewards® customer loyalty program, you collect a Welcome Rewards credit for every night you spend in any participating hotel chain, boutique hotel or bed and breakfast booked through Hotels.com. For every 10 hotel stays, members earn a free night that can be redeemed at more than 85,000 partner hotels, with no restrictions or blackout dates.

Hotels.com

The average daily rate of the ten nights stayed represents the maximum value of the free night. Credits do not expire as long as Welcome Rewards members remain active on their account at least once every 12 months (simply book one stay every year to keep your account active). The free night does not include taxes and fees.

This is one of the easiest loyalty programs to figure out and use if you are not a heavy traveller. I recommend this program to light-travellers that do not want to have loyalty to any hotel chain.

Marriott Rewards®

Marriott Rewards® is the frequent traveler program for the Marriott hotels chain (Marriott Hotels & Resorts, JW Marriott Hotels & Resorts, Gaylord Hotels, Renaissance Hotels, Ritz-Carlton, AC Hotels by Marriott, Autograph Collection Hotels & Resorts, Marriott Conference Centers, Courtyard by Marriott, Fairfield Inn by Marriott, SpringHill Suites® by Marriott, Residence Inn by Marriott, TownePlace Suites by Marriott, Marriott Executive Apartments, Marriott Vacation Club International (MVCI), Marriott Grand Residence Club, The Residences at the Ritz-Carlton, and The Ritz-Carlton Destination Club®).

This program rewards you with exclusive membership privileges when you travel, as well as your choice of frequent flyer miles in your preferred airline program, or points toward free hotels and vacations.

Silver, Gold, and Platinum Elite Status in the Marriott Rewards® program have many benefits.

Silver:

- Elite Reservation line
- Exclusive Guest Services line
- Ultimate Reservation Guarantee
- Silver Exclusive Elite offers
- Priority late checkout
- Weekend discounts (Available at participating Courtyard and SpringHill Suites® locations in the U.S. and Canada)
- Gift shop discount
- 20% bonus on points for stays

Gold:

- Free Internet Access
- Room upgrade
- Guaranteed room type
- Guaranteed lounge access/breakfast

- Free local phone, free local fax and discounted long-distance phone calls (Available only at participating U.S. and Canada locations).
- Hertz #1 Gold Plus Rewards membership
- 25% bonus on points for stays
- Gold customized rewards

Platinum:

- Guaranteed Platinum arrival gift
- 50% bonus on points for stays
- Platinum customized rewards

I have been a Platinum member, and the benefits were incredible for my stays in Seattle, Portugal, and Victoria, BC. I would say one of the better benefits is having access to free Internet, and the lounge access. The lounges I have been to have incredible food for breakfast, and provide hor d'oeuvres in the early evening (usually between 5 and 7 pm). One of the main differences between lounges in North America and Europe is the availability of free alcohol (beer and wine). In North America, the lounges can charge upwards of $10 per glass of wine.

Earn Points for stays

Depending on the Marriott hotel for your stay, you may earn up to 10 points or two air miles for every U.S. dollar spent on your room rate or your total bill.

ShopMyWay Mall

You can earn a considerable amount of Marriott Rewards® points by shopping online through the Marriott ShopMyWay storefront.

Marriott ShopMyWay Mall.

With the ShopMyWay Mall, you simply find the retailer you'd like to shop at, and click through to that retailer's store page. Your purchase will be tracked and you'll be credited with Marriott Rewards® points in a few weeks. I recommend taking a screen shot/print out of the opening merchant screen (which has the partner number), and the amount of your final sale for your documentation in case the points do not get credited.

The mall has primarily United States retailers, but also a number of retailers that are available to Canadians like Groupon, AbeBooks, Brookstone, and iTunes.

Referral Bonus

Refer a friend to Marriott Rewards® and both of you earn 2,000 bonus points per stay. There is a maximum of five stays per referral (10,000 points) and five referrals (50,000 points) per year. A stay is defined as consecutive nights spent in the same hotel, regardless of check-in/check-out activity.

New members who join through the referral program must designate Marriott Rewards® points as their earning preference. If you need a current member to refer you, feel free to send me an email. This offer is valid only for new members.

Travel Package redemptions

Marriott has interesting redemption offers for travelers not just looking at a hotel stay. You can exchange your points for a week of hotel accommodations, and receive airline miles and a 25% Hertz rental-car discount (available at participating locations in the U.S.A .and Europe) included.

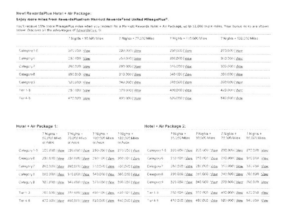

Travel Packages for Marriott Rewards.

For example, you can use 270,000 Marriott Rewards® Points to receive seven nights at a Category 5 resort and receive 120,000 frequent flyer miles of your choice (Aeroplan, Alaska Air, Avios, United, and US Airways).

An example of a Category 5 hotel is the Renaissance Aruba Resort & Casino. A normal Category 5 hotel redemption would cost 25,000 per night, for a total of 150,000 points for seven nights (redeeming for four nights gets the fifth night free). So, this may not look like a good deal, but since you receive 120,000 frequent flyer miles you are achieving a Marriott Rewards® points transfer at a 1 to 1 ratio, instead of the usual 5 to 1.

Transfer Points

You are able to transfer points to your legal spouse or domestic partner at the time of redemption if he or she is also a Rewards member. This is a nice way to combine points to redeem for a larger reward.

PointSavers® Reward Redemptions

Marriott periodically updates this list of hotels that allow you to redeem up to 33% fewer points. Locations participating in PointSavers® are discounted by one category in Marriott Rewards® point requirements. You could find some interesting redemptions if you are flexible with your travel plans.

For example, you can stay in a Category 5 hotel while redeeming points for a Category 4 hotel. So, to stay at a Category 5 hotel for two nights at a standard redemption would require 50,000 Marriott Rewards® points. The same stay with PointSavers® would be 40,000 points, or a 20% savings. Category 1 hotels point requirements are discounted by 20%.

While all brands are eligible to participate, all hotels may not be participating in PointSavers® on all dates. The participating hotels listed on the PointSavers® page are being revised weekly.

Seasonal Awards

Seasonal Awards offer you savings on the points required (25% fewer points) for a free night during certain times of the year.

The Marriott Rewards® Seasonal Awards webpage lists participating properties by U.S. cities and international countries.

A good tip to remember is that you may combine this discount with the Marriott redemption of "redeem four nights, get the fifth night free" offer, meaning that five nights can be had for the price of three.

Use Cash Back websites to book your stay

If you use a cash back website, you will receive up to 2.5% cash back when you book any Marriott property using Ebates.

Cash back is not available on rooms offered at specially negotiated rates, where the customer is required to be affiliated with or employed by a particular company or organization to receive the special rate (e.g., government rate or the Marriott employee rate), and rooms that are booked and paid for using Marriott Rewards® Points.

Using a cash-back website will not affect the price you pay, or any special offers, or points earning.

Use Cash and Points

Marriott Rewards® Cash and Points give you the convenience of combining redemption nights and cash nights when you book online. You will still earn points and Elite night credits for your nights paid with cash. It is another great way to use your points.

SPG (Starwood Preferred Guest®)

Starwood Preferred Guest® (SPG) is the loyalty program for the Starwood hotels chain (Westin, Sheraton, Four Points by Sheraton, W Hotels, Le Meridien, St. Regis, The Luxury Collection, Aloft, and Element).

SPG has a few membership tiers:

1. Preferred

At this entry level you earn two Starpoints® for every eligible U.S. dollar spent, including restaurant and room service charges, in-room movies, and more. You also receive members-only offers so you can save on luxurious getaways, and quickly earn bonus Starpoints® for your stays.

2. Gold

Gold status is reached after completing 10 stays or 25 nights in a calendar year. Both paid stays and Award redemption stays and nights count toward elite status earning. As a Gold member, you receive all the benefits of Preferred, plus these benefits:

- Three Starpoints® for every eligible U.S. dollar spent – a 50% bonus over base-level membership.

- 4 p.m. late checkout.

- An enhanced room at check-in, when available.

- Special Elite customer service telephone line (available in most countries).

- A welcome gift with each stay (choice of bonus Starpoints®, complimentary in-room Internet access and a complimentary beverage).

3. Platinum

Platinum status is reached after completing 25 stays or 50 nights in a calendar year. Both paid stays and Award redemption stays count toward elite status earning. As a Platinum member, you'll receive all the benefits of Preferred, these benefits:

- Three Starpoints® per eligible US dollar spent, a 50% bonus over the Preferred level.

- Upgrades to best available room at check-in, including Standard Suites.

- Welcome gift with each stay (choice of bonus Starpoints®, continental breakfast, and local amenities).

- Club and Executive-level privileges where available.

- Complimentary in-room Internet access.

- Guaranteed room availability when your room is booked by 3 p.m., 72+ hours prior to arrival.

- Special Platinum Concierge service

Earning SPG points

You mainly earn points on stays at Starwood properties but this program has partnerships with over thirty airlines including Aeroplan, Air France/KLM, Alaska, American, ANA, British Airways, Delta, Emirates, Lufthansa, Singapore, US Airways, United, and Virgin Atlantic.

SPG and the Delta SkyMiles® program have created a program called Crossover Rewards (for SPG Elite and Delta Medallion® members). You can earn Starpoints® on all eligible Delta flights. You can even get additional benefits, like your first checked bag free, priority check-in and Priority Boarding with Delta flights for SPG Platinum members.

SPG does not have any online shopping mall or store to earn SPG points. You can earn SPG points using Avis, SIXT Rent a car.

Another major way to earn SPG points is applying and using their affiliate credit card, the Starwood Preferred Guest® Credit Card from American Express. This card usually comes with a bonus of 10,000 SPG points, but that could be as high as 20,000 if you wait for the promotion. You can earn one SPG point for every dollar spent with this card, and it comes with nice travel insurance benefits.

Some Starwood hotels participate in the Green Choice program. This means that if you choose to participate and decline housekeeping you will earn 500 Starpoints® awarded at check out for each night you decline housekeeping services (except day of departure).

Spending SPG points

I consider this hotel rewards program one of the best, because of the flexibility in converting the points to your favourite frequent flyer program, and the generous redemption values.

When redeeming the points that you earn at hotels in the SPG program, no capacity controls or blackout dates are imposed on the use of points. This is a nice advantage over most hotel loyalty programs where it is not possible to get a room for a Super Bowl or New Year's Eve.

You can convert your SPG points at a 1:1 exchange ratio to many major airline frequent flyer programs like Aeroplan, British Airways, American Airlines, and Alaska Airlines. An additional 5,000-mile bonus is awarded if you transfer 20,000 miles at one time. For example, if you had 20,000 SPG points and transferred the points to Aeroplan, you would have 25,000 Aeroplan miles.

SPG has two main redemption types when using the points earned at their properties: the traditional points redemption, and the cash and points redemption.

Points redemption

Starwood's properties cost anywhere from just 2,000 points for a weekend night at a Category 1 hotel property to 35,000 points at a top of the line Category 7 hotel.

	Category 1	Category 2	Category 3	Category 4	Category 5	Category 6	Category 7
Free Night (Redeem 4 nights, get the 5th night free, excludes categories 1 & 2) • Weekdays	3,000	4,000	7,000	10,000	12,000 — 16,000	20,000 — 25,000	30,000 — 35,000
• Weekends	just 2,000	just 3,000	7,000	10,000	12,000 — 16,000	20,000 — 25,000	30,000 — 35,000
Cash & Points • Standard Rooms	1,500 Starpoints + $30	2,000 Starpoints + $35	3,500 Starpoints + $55	6,000 Starpoints + $75	8,000 Starpoints + $110	10,000 Starpoints + $180	16,000 Starpoints + $275
	2,000 — 2,250 Starpoints + $50 — $60	2,500 — 2,750 Starpoints + $55 — $65	4,000 — 4,250 Starpoints + $75 — $85	6,500 — 6,750 Starpoints + $95 — $105	8,750 — 7,250 Starpoints + $135 — $165	10,750 — 11,250 Starpoints + $210 — $230	15,750 — 16,250 Starpoints + $290 — $315
	3,000 Starpoints + $70	4,000 Starpoints + $95	7,000 Starpoints + $120	7,000 Starpoints + $175	12,000 Starpoints + $275	20,000 Starpoints + $450	30,000 Starpoints + $625
Room Upgrade	1,000 — 1,500	1,000 — 1,500	1,000 — 1,500	1,000 — 1,500	1,000 — 2,750	1,000 — 2,750	1,000 — 2,750
Suite Upgrade	3,000	4,000	7,000	10,000	12,000 — 16,000	20,000 — 25,000	30,000 — 35,000
50% off Regular Rack Rates	1,000	1,000	1,000	1,000	1,000	1,000	1,000
Nights & Flights	n/a	n/a	60,000	70,000	n/a	n/a	n/a

Starpoints Hotel Redemption.

You will need 2,000 Starpoints® for a free weekend night and 3,000 Starpoints® for a free night during the week at a Category 1 hotel. The problem is that Starwood does not have many Category 1 hotels in North America.

The Westin Ka'anapali Ocean Resort Villas in Maui, a hotel in the Category 7 class, could cost as much as $339 US per night.

Example of Category 7 Starwood Hotel.

As nice as it may be staying at a Category 7 hotel, the redemption value is quite low. Dividing the points by the cost of the hotel ($339/35,000 SPG points), you get a return of under one cent per SPG point.

I personally believe some of the better redemption values are at hotels in the lower categories. Here is an example of an SPG Category 2 hotel in Fort Lauderdale that would cost 3,000 SPG points for a one-night stay.

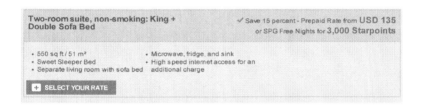

Starwood Category 2 hotel.

Dividing the points by the cost of the hotel in Canadian dollars ($135/3,000 SPG points), you get a return of four and a half cents per SPG point. This would give you quadruple the return of your SPG points at a Category 7 hotel.

Starwood has a nice redemption bonus when you redeem five nights at category 3, 4, 5, 6 and 7 hotels, you get the fifth night free. I recommend that you save your SPG points for a longer period to stretch the value of your points.

Cash and Points Redemption

Starwood also offers a redemption option called Cash and Points, which lets you combine cash and points to pay for a room. Starwood charges different rates of cash and points, depending on the category of the hotel you want to stay in.

For example, in a Category 1 hotel, they charge 1,500 SPG points plus $30. For a Category 4 they charge 5,000 SPG points plus $75. For a Category 7 hotel, they charge you 15,000 SPG points plus $275.

	Category 1	Category 2	Category 3	Category 4	Category 5	Category 6	Category 7
Standard Rooms	1,500 Starpoints + $30	2,000 Starpoints + $35	3,500 Starpoints + $55	5,000 Starpoints + $75	6,000 Starpoints + $110	10,000 Starpoints + $180	15,000 Starpoints + $275
Upgraded Rooms	2,000 — 2,250 Starpoints + $50 — $60	2,500 — 2,750 Starpoints + $55 — $65	4,000 — 4,250 Starpoints + $75 — $85	5,500 — 5,750 Starpoints + $95 — $105	6,750 — 7,250 Starpoints + $135 — $150	10,750 — 11,250 Starpoints + $210 — $230	15,750 — 16,250 Starpoints + $290 — $315
Suites	3,000 Starpoints + $75	4,000 Starpoints + $95	7,000 Starpoints + $125	10,000 Starpoints + $175	12,000 Starpoints + $275	20,000 Starpoints + $450	30,000 Starpoints + $625

SPG Cash & Points redemption chart.

The rooms are based on availability, so it is likely these rates will not be available if the hotel is expecting to be busy. Also, black-out dates apply to these types of redemptions.

Nights & Flights

Starwood lets you use your Starpoints® to pay for your entire vacation — hotel and airfare! They have limited redemption options, and the hotels are only available in Category 3 and 4, but I did see some great deals.

With Nights & Flights, you can redeem 60,000 Starpoints® for 50,000 airline miles and five free nights at a Category 3 hotel or resort.

With Nights & Flights II, you can redeem 70,000 Starpoints® and receive 50,000 airline miles and five free nights at a Category 4 hotel or resort.

Let's break down the first option to see if this is a good return on your Starpoints®.

A Category 3 hotel charges 7,000 Starpoints® for a free night, so a five night stay would cost 28,000 Starpoints® with the fifth night being free. The Nights & Flights redemption costs just 20,000 Starpoints® with you receiving 50,000 airline frequent flyer miles (40,000 + 10,000 bonus transfer). So using Nights & Flights saves you 8,000 Starpoints®, that you can then use for another free night!

A Category 4 hotel charges 10,000 Starpoints® for a free night, so a five night stay would cost 40,000 Starpoints® with the fifth night being free. The Nights & Flights redemption costs just 30,000 Starpoints® with you receiving 50,000 airline frequent flyer miles (40,000 + 10,000 bonus transfer). So using Nights & Flights saves you 10,000 Starpoints®.

Some conditions redeeming Starpoints® for Nights & Flights are:

1. Nights & Flights award redemptions must be made by phone.

2. Nights & Flights Awards must be ordered at least 14 business days prior to the arrival date for a U.S. airline, and at least 30 business days prior to arrival for a non-U.S. airline. This will allow for processing of the airline transfer portion of the award.

3. This Award is only offered with airlines with a 1 Starpoint® to 1 Airline mile transfer ratio. The maximum transfer to the airline offered in this award is 50,000 miles, so it is each member's responsibility to verify with their desired airline the value of these miles for air travel awards.

4. No Starpoints® will be refunded for any portion of the Nights & Flights award's free nights not stayed at the property. Members who elect to stay fewer nights than the required five nights stay for the Nights & Flights award offer should advise the hotel at check-in to avoid any early departure charges.

Nights & Flights awards may be canceled. If a Nights & Flights award is canceled, the member will only receive a Starpoint® credit of 20,000 for a Category 3 and 30,000 for a Category 4.

50% off Regular Rack Rates

You can redeem just 1,000 Starpoints® for a certificate offering 50% off regular rack rates for a stay of up to five nights. You need to redeem over the phone. Unlike Free Nights Awards, 50% Off Regular Rack Rates awards are subject to availability.

These special rates can provide savings at certain properties during certain times of the year. I do not recommend using these certificates for any lower category hotel property. Try to save these for a Category 6 or 7 hotel.

Transfer SPG Starpoints*

SPG lets you combine points with another family member. If you share an address, you can move Starpoints® between accounts. Both accounts must have been active and with the same address on each for at least 30 days. This is a nice way to redeem for a larger redemption.

Redeem for Flights

With SPG Flights, you can redeem Starpoints® to fly on more than 350 airlines, with no blackout dates. You will not find any standard restrictions that limit most frequent-flyer awards. Plus, you can search for airline tickets whenever you choose, even during peak periods such as holidays.

How many Starpoints?

Ticket Price*	Starpoints
up to $150	10,000
$150-$215	15,000
$215-$280	20,000
$280-$345	25,000
$345-$410	30,000
$410-$475	35,000
$475-$540	40,000
$540-$605	45,000
$605-$670	50,000
$670-$735	55,000
$735-$800	60,000
$800-$865	65,000
$865-$930	70,000
$930-$995	75,000
$995-$1060	80,000
Higher prices (examples)	
$2,880-$3,140	235,000
$4,960-$5,220	395,000
$9,900-$10,160	775,000

Need more Starpoints?
Buy now

*Ticket Price includes Taxes &
Fees. Baggage fees may apply.

SPG Flights redemption chart.

The total U.S. dollar amount of the flight is converted to Starpoints® as listed on the redemption chart. The amount is based on the fare plus tax required by the airlines as listed in the Worldspan Global Distribution System (GDS) which is used by SPG Flights as well as many travel agencies. Added to the base fare and tax is a $15 USD booking fee, so the final ticket price used to convert to Starpoints® is the total of the cost to the airlines, and the booking fee for the service.

How the program works is that if you find a flight that costs $150 or less, you will need to redeem 10,000 Starpoints®.

I personally would ignore using this redemption, as it has one of the worst returns on a Starpoint® (1.5 cents per Starpoint®).

Pay attention to Partner transfer bonuses

Starwood lets you transfer your points to many frequent flyer programs at a 1:1 ratio, and usually for every 20,000 points you transfer, you earn a 5,000 point bonus.

Occasionally, some programs give transfer bonuses on top of the regular 5,000 bonus. For example, last year American Airlines offered a 35% transfer bonus and US Airways offered a 50% transfer bonus, earning you almost two miles per SPG point. So if you can transfer to an airline during a promotion, by all means do!

Chapter 8

Alternative Hotel Options

I love to stay at hotels, but the costs can add up if you have a larger family or travel to expensive cities. If you don't want to stay in a hotel or are on a low-budget, you still have a number of options. Here are some great alternatives to staying at hotels that will stretch your travel dollars.

Airbnb

Founded in August of 2008 and based in San Francisco, California, Airbnb is a community marketplace for people to list, discover, and book unique accommodations around the world.

Airbnb

Whether you are looking for an apartment for a night, a castle for a week, or a villa for a month, Airbnb connects you to unique travel experiences, at any price point, in more than 33,000 cities and 192 countries.

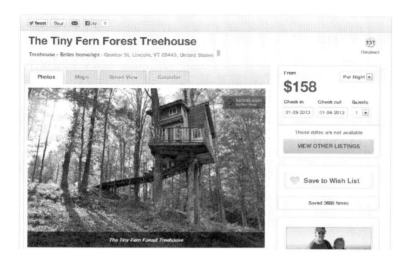

Airbnb listing – The Tiny Fern Forest Treehouse

Airbnb does not perform background checks on users, but they have a number of features to build trust and safety on the site. The website can verify your phone number or connect to Facebook, Twitter, and LinkedIn to add to your profile.

It is a really easy website to use. Simply search for a city and the dates you are looking to stay, and you will see available listings similar to a hotel website.

What I like most about an Airbnb search, as opposed to a regular hotel search, are the filters available for a search.

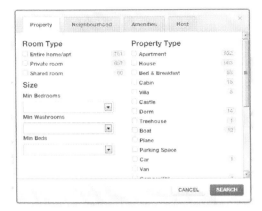

Property filter for Airbnb.

Filters for Airbnb search.

Neighbourhood filter for Airbnb.

After finding a listing that you are interested in, you contact the host by clicking the Contact Me button below their profile photo. You can ask any questions you might have, and confirm availability prior to booking. I recommend messaging multiple hosts. Your personal contact info is kept private until after your reservation has been made, to protect your privacy and keep you safe.

When you send a message to a host, they can pre-approve your stay, and even make you a special offer. If you receive one of these offers in a message, clicking Book It will take you straight to the payment form, and confirm your reservation right away.

What I like about Airbnb is that after your host accepts your reservation, you will be charged for the stay. However, Airbnb will hold on to your money until 24 hours after your check in date, giving you an opportunity to see your accommodations and make sure they're up to scratch. Airbnb collects between six and 12 percent of the total fare as a service fee.

Become an Airbnb host

If you want to make your travel dollars go further, consider becoming an Airbnb host. I have hosted several times, and have earned over one thousand dollars. I only make my home available when we are planning to go on holidays, or are available to leave for a weekend getaway.

Airbnb makes it really easy to generate some income from a spare room or your house when you are away. Airbnb even offers free professional photography to hosts in many cities. The photographer comes to your house, and takes high quality professional images. Professionally photographed listings get booked more often. It was incredible seeing the impact the high-quality photographs do for the listing.

Airbnb charges hosts three percent of the per-night rate for every booking, and collects between six and 12 percent of the total fare from the guest. You do not pay a monthly or annual fee to list your space for rent.

Here are some of my tips to be a good host:

- Read the official Airbnb hosting manual.
- Always communicate with the guest prior to the stay, and be available to your email in case any issues come up.
- Have maps, tourist coupons, and some basic guides to your city for the guest to use.
- Write a personal letter (not e-mail) that shares information about the house, cool restaurants, or interesting things to do in the area.

Hostels

A hostel is a budget oriented accommodation that offers a comfortable night's sleep at an affordable price. Hostels provide the perfect way to get to know a locale at a low cost and meet with many other people who share a common attitude towards travelling.

Inside a hostel, you will find communal facilities such as a common room, a self-catering kitchen, bar, restaurants, library, TV room, laundry facilities, and Internet access. Hostels are not just for singles or couples, and private rooms are available for families.

The majority of hostels have lockers or safes in rooms where you can leave your valuables. Some may require you to have your own padlock or hire/purchase one from reception. Those hostels which do not have the locker facilities in the room usually have a reception safe in which they allow guests to leave their valuables.

There are several major differences between hostels and hotels:

- Hostels tend to be budget-oriented, so the rates charged are considerably lower.

- A person staying at a hotel will have his bags carried to his room, fresh towels delivered, and his bed made up daily, but none of this is likely to be included in a hostel stay.

- For those who prefer an informal environment, hostels do not usually have the same level of formality as hotels.

- Hostels are generally more **adventure travel** oriented than **leisure travel** oriented, thus attracting a younger, more venturesome crowd.

- Hostels may also have strict rules (curfew, lights out, no access during the day).

If you are looking at staying at several hostels over a long period of time, I recommend getting a membership with Hostelling International. A membership with Hostelling International lets you take advantage of discounted member prices in many places around the world and enjoy discounted overnight prices at many hostels. You get a minimum 10% discount at every Hostelling International hostel, plus savings on all kinds of extras like bus trips, food, gear, and activities.

WWOOF

WWOOF (World Wide Opportunities on Organic Farms) was founded in 1971 in the United Kingdom, and is one of the world's first voluntourism and ecotourism organizations.

WWOOF

From the UK, WWOOF spread to Australia, New Zealand, and then Canada in 1985, and now exists in over 100 countries around the world. WWOOF is a help exchange linking volunteers with organic growers, and helps people share more sustainable ways of living.

Flying Shoe Farm, Stanley, New Brunswick, Canada

WWOOF is a help exchange - in return for volunteer help, WWOOF hosts offer food, accommodation and opportunities to learn about organic lifestyles.

They recommend that volunteers have a genuine interest in learning about organic growing, country living, or ecologically sound lifestyles. They also need to help their hosts with daily tasks for an agreed number of hours. You help 4-6 hours a day, 5 - 5 1/2 days per week and receive accommodations, meals and a very interesting experience.

Before you can start applying for opportunities, you need to pay a fee to register with the various WWOOF websites around the world (Canada, US, Europe, Latin America). You can preview the list prior to becoming a member, but the preview is quite limited.

Couchsurfing

Couchsurfing.org is a community of over 5 million members around the world. The website connects travelers and locals who meet offline to share cultures, hospitality, and adventures – whether on the road or in their hometowns.

Getting started with Couchsurfing

Start by building your Couchsurfing profile. This profile is important because it lets potential hosts learn more about you and trust you before meeting. Take some time building a profile and adding a few photos.

This website allows your profile to be verified. The first way to be verified is via credit card verification (approx. $26 for a Canadian address). You'll be mailed a postcard with a code that you can enter to be verified. Another way to get verified is with references from fellow Couchsurfing users. You can join local activities and meetups with other users to see if you can find others to vouch for you.

Before you start looking for a couch, you should build some connections in the Couchsurfing community. You can find a list of upcoming Activities on your dashboard. An example could be a hike or bike ride or concert.

When you start to look for opportunities to Couchsurf, make sure that you leave enough time to communicate with the host.

Houseswapping

Have you ever considered doing a house swap? Basically, you stay in someone's home while they stay in yours. Usually this is a barter transaction where no cash changes hands.

House swapping works best when you have an appealing place to offer, and you can live with the idea of having strangers in your home. So you do not need to have an upscale condo or a country home in cottage country, but these locations will have the pick of the better options in other countries.

I enjoy staying at nice hotels, but there is something to be said for staying at a house. I have done four house swaps to save money on hotels and eating out while traveling, and they were all amazing experiences.

I am based in Victoria, British Columbia on Vancouver Island, and my family and I have had great experiences spending time with different people.

Our first house swap was in Albuquerque, New Mexico for the famous Hot Air Balloon festival. We stayed in a couple's 1,000 square foot extension to their house. The extension was two stories with a gorgeous soaker tub, leather sofa, king-sized bed, and kitchen that enabled us to save money.

We did another house swap to another island in British Columbia, Saltspring Island, where accommodation would have been expensive due to a lack of supply demand problem in the summer.

Finally, each year we do a house swap with a couple in Long Beach, Washington, who have a gorgeous vacation home on the ocean with two cruiser bicycles and a king-sized bed. It was a nice treat to see two 50" high-definition televisions, and a lovely kitchen and barbeque to prepare our fresh seafood.

What I like about house swapping is the fact that you become good friends with the people that you are swapping with. All of the house swaps I have done were found using Craigslist in the Housing Swap category under Housing. Once I found a potential host, I made sure that I had a good list of questions to ask. I had several conversations with the other party regarding the expectations I had, and questions on their house. After a few successful house swaps, I felt that I was not staying at a stranger's house, but at a friend's house.

In the Tools area at the end of the chapter, I have included some great places to start looking for house swaps.

Housesitting

Housesitting is the practice whereby the homeowner leaves their house for a period of time, and entrusts it to one or more house sitters. The housesitter and homeowner create a mutual agreement where the housesitter is entitled to live rent-free in exchange for assuming responsibilities, such as taking care of the homeowner's pets, performing general maintenance (including pools, lawns, air-conditioning systems etc.), sorting the mail, and general maintenance of the home. Housesitting is an option for those travelers looking to travel, but who may not have enough money for accommodation.

If you've never house-sat before, I recommend getting references from your family, friends, and work colleagues. Once you have a few good experiences and references, you can then register on the various housesitting websites available to seek opportunities to housesit around the world. All these websites require you to fill out your profile as thoroughly as possible, giving as much information about yourself, why you want to housesit, and what you can offer as a house sitter. I always recommend adding your photo to your profile to give as much reassurance as possible to the homeowner.

Housesitting tips

1. Make sure that you have an attractive profile. Think of this as your resume. This is what the potential home owners will see, so make sure your profile is well written and recent. Include items like:

- Previous experience in house sitting or if you are a current or previous home owner.

- Show that you can take care of pets. You will find that the large majority of house sitting jobs include pet care.

- If you can speak other languages or have experience in gardening or lawn care, include them in your profile.

2. When applying for any house sitting job, make sure you share all the important information about yourself, and try to demonstrate that you are enthusiastic to take on this job.

3. Prepare your house sitting references in advance. Make sure that you have reliable references that will vouch for you. If you have no prior house sitting experience, look at people like former landlords, neighbours, or your employer.

Tools

- AirBnb - http://www.canadiantravelhacking.com/go/airbnb/

- Hostelling International – http://www.hihostels.ca/

- WWOOF Canada – http://www.wwoof.ca/

- Couchsurfing International - https://www.couchsurfing.org/

- HomeExchange.com – http://www.homeexchange.com/

- HomeLink.ca – http://www.homelink.ca/

- Intervac Canada – http://www.intervac.ca/

- Trusted House Sitters - http://www.trustedhousesitters.com

- HouseCarers.com - http://www.housecarers.com/

- MindMyHouse - http://www.mindmyhouse.com/

Section 3: Transportation

Chapter 9

Car Rentals

Renting a car can be expensive, but if you know some of the workarounds to the high-pressure sales agents when booking, you can save some money.

Name your own price with Priceline

I am a big advocate of using Priceline.com for renting cars. I don't care if the brand is Alamo®, Avis®, Budget®, National®, Hertz®, or Thrifty®. Personally, the lowest rate is the deciding factor for my car rental.

Some of the discount car rental companies do not appear on Priceline's listings, like Advantage or Payless. Make sure when you bid that you are positive that your plans will not change because you cannot cancel or modify a Priceline **Name Your Own Price**® reservation. You also cannot use this Priceline® method to rent cars at non-airport locations and for a one-way rental.

Before I start bidding, I want to make sure that I have an existing car rental reservation. The reason for this is that as soon as I have an accepted bid, I am able to cancel my reservation.

Make sure that you click from a cash-back shopping website like Ebates® or Great Canadian Rebates. These websites will provide you with an additional discount.

Receive 3% cash back on Name your Price Rental Cars through Ebates.

Now because Priceline® doesn't tell you how much to bid, you need to have a good baseline to start. The price for a car rental in Orlando, Florida for one week will be different from a car rental for three days in Red Deer, Alberta. I like to use websites like Expedia® or Hotwire® to see how much rentals are for the days I am looking for.

Here is a sample search for a car rental in San Diego using Expedia®. For a mid-size vehicle, the prices range from $211.80 with Advantage to $467.24 with National®, a difference of over $255 dollars. Using this data, I can prepare a better starting bid with Priceline®.

The parameters for a Priceline® car rental search are simple: the price per day you are willing to pay, type of car, location, and dates. You also have the option to add infant car seats. I started with a low-ball offer of $11 per day for a mid-size car. I will always start with a low starting price, because this potential reservation cannot be cancelled or changed using Priceline®. Based on my history of prior bids, I recommend starting with a bid that is 20-25% lower than what is available on Expedia® or other car rental reservation websites.

If your bid is not accepted, Priceline® will sometimes come back with an offer, or just ask you to re-bid.

Priceline® limits your bids to one per 24 hours. One way around this limit is to bid again on a different sized-car. I previously bid $17 for a full-size car, but increasing my bid at $18 for a larger vehicle gives me a free re-bid.

Three things to remember when using Priceline*

1. If you need to change your plans, you're stuck, as your purchase is both non-refundable and non-changeable.

2. Taxes and car rental fees are not included in your bid, so keep this in mind for your bid.

3. You will not earn any frequent flyer miles for your car rental.

Extra fees Car Rental Companies charge

When you receive your final statement, you will see many additional charges and taxes that were not in the original cost. This way, car rental companies can charge low rates, but pass extra costs to its customers in additional fees and taxes.

Here is a breakdown of some of the more common charges:

Additional Driver Fee

This is the fee that the car rental company charges to have an additional driver that did not make the reservation. Each car rental chain handles this charge differently. Some companies allow a spouse or an immediate family member to drive at no additional cost.

If you rent in certain states like California, you will not have to pay this fee (it is against the law there). Ask the company prior to the rental about their policy. Some companies may waive this fee if you are a loyalty member (member of Hertz®, Alamo®, or National®), or belong to CAA.

Make sure you do not let another person drive the rental car without paying this fee. If they have an accident, the insurance coverage for the vehicle would not cover them, as the contract is for the legal driver of the vehicle only.

Airport Concession Recovery Fee

If you rented your car at an airport location, you will often see this fee depending on the airport. This is the fee charged to the car rental company by the airport for every transaction. This charge is passed to the customer.

To avoid this fee, investigate picking up and dropping off your car at an off-airport location. Ask the rental car company for options prior to booking, as this fee can be quite high, depending on the location.

Frequent Flyer Fee

This is a small fee, usually from $0.50 to $2 per day, but it is what the car rental company charges you for the privilege of collecting frequent flyer miles from your car rental. You do not earn a lot of miles from each rental (usually around 50 miles per day unless you get a bonus). However, if you see a promotion with your frequent flyer program, it may be worthwhile to pay the fee.

Transportation fee

In larger airports, car rental companies share a location and shuttle bus service to provide convenient pick-up and drop-off from the airport terminal. This fee to provide this service is passed on to you from the car rental company.

Tourism tax

Several states and counties in the United States charge this tax to improve infrastructure (highways or a convention center). This can be a single flat fee or a per-day charge.

Vehicle registration fee

This car rental fee is charged to renters for vehicle registration and licensing fees.

Search for coupon codes or discounts available.

Car rental companies have many coupon codes easily available. If you are a member of any frequent flyer program or Costco® or CAA, you are also eligible for car rental discounts. Check with your Human Resources department to see if your company is entitled to a special discount with a car rental company. The trade association or union that you are a member of can be entitled to a discount.

Search on Google for terms like **Hertz coupon code** or **Hertz promotion code**.

Use AutoSlash.com

This website finds all the best coupons and discount codes for car rentals. After you book using their website, they analyze your rental, and figure out how to lower your rate even more. If they find a better deal, they will automatically re-book you to lock in the savings. It's like price protection for your rental.

How to land free upgrades

One nice trick I have when renting a car is to always downgrade your rental when you book. This means booking a mid-size or compact when you want a full-size. My experience is that at the counter, the agent will always try to give you a free upgrade or when you go to the lot to pick up your car, they will give you another one much large. On a recent trip to Fort Lauderdale, I was given a huge minivan for the price of a mid-size.

So if you are looking for a full-size car, consider reserving a mid-size car. If the rental agency has sold out of the requested size of the vehicle, you usually get the upgrade for free.

It is usually cheaper to negotiate at the rental car counter, as they have more leeway to negotiate.

Avoid the pre-purchase gas option

This is one of the biggest upsells at the car rental counter. The customer service agent will try to explain that pre-paying for your gas saves you time and money. However, they fail to point out that the prepaid gas price is usually higher than the average price you can get from local gas stations near the rental office.

Another thing to remember is that, unless you leave the tank close to empty, you are not saving time or money.

Make sure you return the car with a full-tank

If you choose to decline the pre-payment option for the gas for your car rental, make sure that you return the car with a full tank of gas. If you do not, expect to pay a high premium (sometimes two to three times the actual price).

Join the loyalty programs

Even if you do not rent often, joining the loyalty program of each major rental car company has its benefits.

Depending on the company, the best benefits are the automated kiosks for loyalty members. Using your loyalty card, you print out your contract, and head to the parking lot for your rental car. This is a major time saver, as I have waited over an hour at times in some busy airports.

Alamo Insiders

This is a free program to join. Alamo Insiders are guaranteed at least a 10% discount on their retail rates. When a promotional rate is available that surpasses 10% off retail rates, you will automatically receive the promotional rate instead of the percentage discount. These special discounts can't be combined with other discounts or coupons.

Alamo Insiders members don't have to pay an additional driver fee in most cases. The members' spouse, common law spouse, or domestic partner who has the same address on the driver's license as the member, and who meet normal renter requirements, will not have to pay the usual extra $10 a day fee.

At popular airports like Orlando, you will find self-serve kiosks that will save you time with the paper-work involved.

With no cost involved with becoming an Alamo Insider, there is absolutely no reason why you shouldn't sign up for it to make your rental go a little smoother, and to possible save some money.

Emerald Club

This is the loyalty program for Enterprise Rent-a-Car®.

Some of the benefits include:

- Free rental days on any car, any day with no blackout dates (must have at least one qualifying Enterprise® rental during every two-year period).
- Members-only check-in at participating locations.
- A dedicated phone number for expedited service.
- Special offers when you subscribe to Email Extras at enterprise.com.

Blue Chip Express Rental Program

This is the Thrifty® loyalty program. Similar to other car rental loyalty programs they have a special Blue Chip Members Only line so you can get on the road faster.

One nice benefit is that your preferences are stored online, so you can return and book faster. It is a simple program in that for every 16 days that you rent, you'll earn one free day.

Hertz®

This program lets you skip the counter at over 40 airports. At over 1,000 off-airport locations worldwide, you just go to the designated Gold counters, show your driver's license and pick up your keys.

Members enjoy:

- Members' only discounts.
- Save on the additional driver fee when your spouse or domestic partner travels with you (save $13 a day per driver).
- Pay less on the rental of infant and/or child seats.
- Earn one Hertz Gold Plus Rewards™ point for every qualifying dollar spent, plus bonuses.

Costco discounts

If you are a Costco® member, you get extra discounts at Avis® and Budget®, depending on if you are an Executive or Gold member. Discounts range from up to 25 % coupon codes, free car upgrades, and no surcharges for a primary driver 21-24 years of age.

Try discount car rental brands

Have you heard of car rental chains Fox Rent a Car or Sixt?

These chains have lower operating costs than the mainstream car rental companies. Fox has seventeen major airport locations across the United States, and has been in business since 1989. Sixt is based in Germany, and has been operating since 1912.

CAA discounts

CAA is affiliated with Hertz® and provides incredible discounts for its members.

CAA member benefits include:
- Up to 20% off daily, weekend, weekly, and monthly rentals.
- No charge for additional qualified CAA drivers, a savings of $13 per day per driver.
- $6.99 per day for Hertz NeverLost® GPS rental, a savings of $6 per day.
- Free use of a child, infant or booster seat, a savings of $11.99 per day.

- Free Hertz Gold Plus Rewards™ plus membership and bonus points.
- 50% off SiriusXM™ Satellite Radio rental, a savings of $2.50 per day.

To receive discounts and benefits, CAA members must provide proof of membership at time of rental by presenting a valid CAA membership card.

Save money on car rental insurance

One of the frustrating things about renting a car is the sales pitch at the counter. This is challenging, because the agent goes over everything so quickly, and shows many legal documents that can be overwhelming.

If you own a major credit card, you should have a collision damage waiver (CDW) supplement or loss damage waiver (LDW) supplement insurance included for free if you rent your car with your credit card.

Make sure that you call your credit card company prior to declining this insurance with the car rental company. My Visa credit card had stipulations:

- The vehicle could not be worth more than $65,000 Canadian.
- Rental could be no longer than 30 days.
- The insurance only applied to passenger cars, minivans, and SUVs.
- The rental must be paid with the credit card.

In speaking with my credit card company, they recommended that I look closely at the theft insurance offered by the credit card company. The theft of the vehicle would be covered by my credit card, however, the contents would not be. In other words, if I left a brand new iPad or laptop in the car and it was stolen, it would not be covered by the standard insurance.

Standard windshield damage, tires, scratches, and dents were all covered by the credit card with no deductible.

My credit card company also recommended that I look at acquiring liability insurance. Very rarely is it included in the price of the rental by the rental agency.

I recommend looking at how much roadside assistance is for the car rental, as opposed to using CAA.

Rent off-airport if possible

I recommend looking for a car rental company that is having a sale in your destination market, or at least the company with the lowest current rates. Check if the company has an off airport rental office that is closest to the airport terminal.

Consider if the difference in rates at the airport pays for cab fare and inconvenience

To estimate cab fares for major cities, search for a Web site such as TaxiFareFinder.com, or look at mass transit options. Cab fare often proves more practical, unless you have the good fortune of finding a car rental office next to a subway or bus stop.

Remember, the more days you keep the rental, the more important it will become to employ this strategy. Don't pay too much for airport car rental convenience.

Tools

- Priceline - http://www.canadiantravelhacking.com/go/priceline-cars

- Expedia – http://www.canadiantravelhacking.com/go/expedia

- Ebates - http://www.canadiantravelhacking.com/go/ebates

- Great Canadian Rebates - http://www.canadiantravelhacking.com/go/gcr

- CAA - http://www.caa.ca/

- Alamo Insiders - http://www.canadiantravelhacking.com/go/alamo

- AutoSlash - http://www.AutoSlash.com/

- Emerald Club - http://www.canadiantravelhacking.com/go/emerald-club

- Blue Chip Express - http://www.canadiantravelhacking.com/go/blue-chip-express

- Hertz - http://www.canadiantravelhacking.com/go/hertz

Section 4: Cruises

Chapter 10

Cruising

My wife and I enjoy taking cruises, and find it a good way to travel frugally. After taking a Mediterranean cruise for our honeymoon, we were amazed at how far our vacation budget with a cruise.

A cruise offers a choice of dining options, and world-class entertainment.

The way we see it is that the accommodation and food is taken care of, and we get to see new places every day when we are not at sea. It is a stress-less vacation for us.

Cruise companies like Carnival®, Norwegian Cruise Lines®, and Royal Caribbean® will often have cruises that will go to the Caribbean, Europe, Alaska, and Hawaii. You will find cruises that go all sorts of places in the world.

This chapter will share my tips and tricks to make cruising more affordable, and what to look out for.

Take a Repositioning Cruise

Cruise lines reposition their ships from Alaska to the warmer weather of the Caribbean and Mexico in the fall, and then move them back to Alaska in the late spring. Most cruise ships that spend their summers in Europe will cross the Atlantic in the late fall to spend the winter months in the Caribbean, and then reverse the process the next spring. Other ships traveling to Asia, South America, Africa, or Australia will also often reposition to other parts of the world when the weather changes.

All of these repositioning cruises are usually 10 days or longer, and most feature numerous days at sea. Cruise lines sell these one-way routes at a significant discount, rather than sail the ships without passengers. Most repositioning cruises are longer compared to the typical cruise, due to the distances they need to cover, but you will end up paying much less than for an average cruise.

Some problems with taking a repositioning cruise are that sailing this type of cruise requires one-way or open-jaw flights, and that these cruises will make fewer port visits.

Here are some sample repositioning cruises and prices:

Cruise Line	Itinerary	Dates	Price
Royal Caribbean	*15 nights Barcelona to New Orleans*	November 2013	$749
Norwegian Cruise Lines	*12 nights Copenhagen to Miami*	October 2013	$554
Carnival Cruises	*15 nights Tampa to Barcelona*	April 2013	$949
Carnival Cruises	*15 nights Dover to New York*	September 2013	$1,189
Carnival Cruises	*15 nights Vancouver to Long Beach*	September 2013	$919

Advanced Booking

On a previous cruise I took, the sales team had a promotion to launch the debut of a new ship, MSC Divina. For the price of an Oceanview stateroom, you would receive a balcony stateroom.

Many cruise lines are looking to get future cruises booked, so they will give on-board credit as a bonus for pre-paying for a future cruise.

If you are able to reserve six to twelve months ahead of your cruise, you can lock in an early-bird rate that's 25 to 50 percent lower than the **published brochure rate** most lines advertise. You will also have a wider selection of itineraries, dates and cabins, and possibly get better deals on airfare and hotels. If prices go down after you book, a good travel agent should help you get the new lower rate.

Additionally, to encourage cruise passengers to book their next cruise holiday, each line will usually have a promotion on-board that gives certain dollars of on-board credit for a deposit for a future sailing. On the last cruise I took, Norwegian Cruise Lines was awarding $100 of on-board credit to use on the current cruise for a $250 deposit for a cruise to be taken within four years.

Late Booking

One of the best times to find last minute rates on a particular sailing is 60 to 90 days prior to departure. The reason for this is that this time is the last call (for most cruise lines and itineraries for some, it's up to 120 days) for travelers to cancel existing reservations without penalty. At that point, the cruise line will know exactly how many cabins are left -- and if there is more space available than the cruise line would like, it will quickly (and often heavily) reduce the fare so that it can sell out the ship.

Join a Cruise Club

Did you know that many cruise lines have rewards programs with valuable savings for cruises booked?

MSC Cruises

The MSC Club is free with various levels of membership. A MSC Club Membership level and privileges grow easily, where you earn points for every night stay plus every 200 Euro spent on board (excluding casino).

You can join the MSC Club after your first sailing. A Classic Card is awarded for just one point and a Silver Card for 22 points and a Gold Card for 43 points.

A Classic membership gives discounts on future cruises (5%), laundry service (20%), mini bar (20%), logo shop, and welcome cocktail party.

Carnival Cruises

The Carnival® loyalty program is called Very Important Fun Person (VIFP). For every day you sail with Carnival®, you earn one VIFP point. If you sail a 7-day Alaska cruise, you earn seven VIFP points.

There are five levels in the VIFP Club. Blue, for first-timers, followed by Red, Gold, Platinum, and the top level, Diamond, all determined by how many days you've cruised.

You earn benefits like collectible Carnival® items, invitations to members-only cocktail receptions, priority boarding, and more.

Norwegian Cruise Lines°

Latitudes Rewards is Norwegian Cruise Line®'s loyalty program for past guests. Receive complimentary enrollment once you complete your first Norwegian cruise. The more times you sail with them, the more benefits you will receive.

Members enjoy exclusive onboard benefits, special offers and more.

Find Agents that will price-match.

If you are looking to book with a reputable travel agent like Expedia Cruise Centers or Flight Centre, often they will price-match. A benefit is the loyalty points gained using these services.

Cruise Compete

This website lets you pit travel agents against each other to offer you a better price. CruiseCompete makes it easy for you to get competing quotes from high-volume cruise travel agencies to help you get the best deal on your next cruise.

Once a cruise sailing is chosen, CruiseCompete users provide brief information, including the number of passengers, and the types of cabins they are interested in, and then submit a quote request. Each request is immediately accessible to more than 300 CruiseCompete member travel agencies. Live agents view the consumer requests and respond with quotes in the system. Users are notified via e-mail each time a new quote is submitted, and provided with a link to their account to view the responses.

All responses are displayed on the same screen and are shown with all taxes, charges, and included bonus extras (on-board credit and excursion discounts). Most requests receive 4-6 responses from agents, along with agent contact information, agency background,and consumer ratings of agency performance. Consumers remain anonymous until they choose to contact a specific agency via phone or e-mail to ask questions or to book their vacations. Most bookings are made via telephone with a live travel agent.

You can have up to three requests being processed at one time, enabling you to compare various cruise lines and itineraries as well.

A recent quote we received was for $1,250 for a 10-day Mediterranean cruise for our family of three (including our baby), with all port taxes.

Sample CruiseCompete request

Sample quote using CruiseCompete

1. Create a new quote request with CruiseCompete.com by naming the cruise ship that you are looking to sail on with information on the cabins and passenger information.

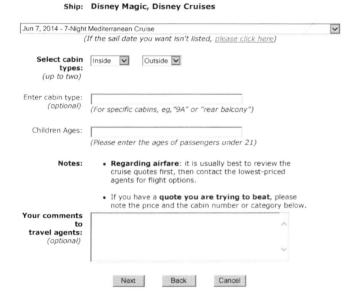

Create New Quote Request

Ship: **Disney Magic, Disney Cruises**

Jun 7, 2014 - 7-Night Mediterranean Cruise

(If the sail date you want isn't listed, please click here)

Select cabin types:
(up to two)

Inside   Outside

Enter cabin type:
(optional)

(For specific cabins, eg,"9A" or "rear balcony")

Children Ages:

(Please enter the ages of passengers under 21)

Notes:
- **Regarding airfare:** it is usually best to review the cruise quotes first, then contact the lowest-priced agents for flight options.
- If you have a **quote you are trying to beat**, please note the price and the cabin number or category below.

Your comments to travel agents:
(optional)

Next   Back   Cancel

Sample CruiseCompete.com Request Step One.

2. For the next step, prepare the sail date, cabin type request, if you were a prior passenger, and at the bottom state any comments to travel agents. If you have a current quote you would like to see beat, add that quote and other information.

Create New Quote Request

Ship: Disney Magic, Disney Cruises

Jun 7, 2014 - 7-Night Mediterranean Cruise	⌄

(If the sail date you want isn't listed, please click here)

Select cabin types:
(up to two)
[Inside ⌄]   [Outside ⌄]

Enter cabin type:
(optional)
[   ]
(For specific cabins, eg, "9A" or "rear balcony")

Children Ages:
[   ]
(Please enter the ages of passengers under 21)

Notes:
- **Regarding airfare**: it is usually best to review the cruise quotes first, then contact the lowest-priced agents for flight options.
- If you have a **quote you are trying to beat**, please note the price and the cabin number or category below.

Your comments to travel agents:
(optional)
[   ]

[Next]   [Back]   [Cancel]

Sample CruiseCompete.com Request Step Two.

3.   Finally, verify your quote request, and click Submit.

I have found in booking two recent cruises that the prices are very competitive, and you will see a dramatic range in prices between companies. In this particular request, I received a range from $1,434.41 to $1,751.03 for an inside cabin to $1,474.78 to $1,771.03 for an ocean view cabin. Each company had various offers ranging from free travel insurance, discount excursions, on-board credit, and a coupon book valued at $300. The quote includes all port charges, taxes, standard delivery of documents, and agency fees.

I have personally used CruiseCompete.com for my last three sailings, and was impressed with the service and savings from the travel agents.

Beware of Taxes

One of the frustrations of travel for many people is the small asterisk that appears on prices.

When booking a cruise until you actually register or phone someone, it is difficult to find the final price of a cruise.

Did you know you could cruise for free?

If you can convince a group of friends to cruise together, you could cruise for free as a **group planner**. Cruise lines reward group planners who organize a trip of at least 16 people (two to a cabin) with a free cruise.

Another way you can cruise for free is by becoming a **Cruise Ship Lecturer**. All cruise ships I have been on have had guest lecturers. If you are a great public speaker with knowledge and passion about a topic, lecturing on a cruise ship is a great way to see the world.

Cruise Ship lecturers fall into two categories: destination lecturers, who present topics related to the ship's itinerary, and enrichment lecturers, who may talk about anything else the cruise line thinks the passengers will find interesting. Duties typically include giving two or three 45-minute presentations a week. The Tools area at the end of the chapter includes several companies that look for lecturers for the cruise lines.

Excursions

Parts of the fun in taking a cruise are the excursions that let you experience everything from going in a submarine to snorkelling and sailing adventures. There are a number of ways of booking an excursion for a cruise: with the cruise line, with a private company, or even independently.

Using the cruise line

The cruise line will provide the widest selection of excursions and they are billed directly to your stateroom. Some reasons why you should book with the cruise line is that the ship will wait for you if your tour is late getting back, guaranteed. I also like the fact that I can ask the shore excursion desk more questions prior to the excursion. You will pay more for this added convenience, as booking with the cruise line is the most expensive option.

Using a private company

The second way of booking excursions is through a private company. A website I recommend using is Viator.com. This website allows you to find what the cruise ships are charging prior to the voyage, and guarantees you the lowest price. This website offers a low-price guarantee.

If you find a lower price for the same tour or activity offered by the same operator (priced in the same currency) within 72 hours of booking, send them the details, and they will refund the price difference.

I have noticed that the cruise line often will have more selection of possible excursions than the private companies.

Book independently

Finally, you have the option to avoid the middleman, and simply book in port after you get off the ship. This is usually how I book excursions, as many depend on the weather, and I enjoy making decisions on the spur of the moment.

Depending on the port, as soon as you get off the ship, you will see many vendors and tour operators with signs offering everything from jet ski rentals, snorkeling, diving, beach days, swimming with dolphins, and island tours. I have found that many vendors are flexible on price.

One of the problems with booking by yourself is that you have no guarantee of getting back to the ship on time. If your tour is late, you are straight out of luck. However, this does not happen often. Also, be careful, not all tour operators are licensed by the local government.

Which way of booking is best for you

If you are looking for a good price and the highest quality excursions, then using a private company would probably be best for you. If you like to decide at the last minute and are looking for the best possible deal, then booking your excursions in port would probably suit you best.

While you may wish to sign up for some of the ship's tours (particularly if you're not familiar with the port and do not speak the language), remember that you always have the option to tour independently at a fraction of the cost -- or even for free, if you go on a self-guided walking tour. Before setting sail, request free planners with maps, calendars of events, and attraction brochures for the ports of call on your itinerary from tourist boards. Check out books on your destination from the public library, and visit websites, to get ideas on things to see.

Parks, beaches, and art galleries showcasing local work are other free or nominal-charge attractions to check out. Or, perhaps you prefer to simply wander through town, browsing in shops and stopping for a coffee or snack.

If you decide to hire a car and driver to give you a private tour (generally less expensive than the shipboard excursions, especially if you have a group), or just to take you to the center of town, always agree on the price (and, in the case of a tour, which specific points of interest will be covered), before you get into the car.

However, many love the security and ease of going through the cruise line, even though the prices are highest. Whichever you choose, enjoy your time in port as you experience and learn about the local culture.

Add the gratuity to your budget

Before you go and book your cruise, remember that most cruise lines have automatic gratuities where each passenger is automatically charged a gratuity that is shared among stateroom stewards, wait staff, buffet stewards, galley staff, laundry staff, and others.

This is usually a set amount like $10-12 per day but if you are taking a 10-day cruise it will increase your cruise budget.

Are you a Shareholder?

Carnival Cruises® gives its investors a little spending money once aboard. They offer $50 in onboard credit for sailings of six days or less, $100 for sailings that are 7 to 13 days long, and $250 for sailings of two weeks or longer. They own the brands Costa Cruises, Princess Cruises®, and Holland American Line®.

The onboard credit can't be used in the casino or for gratuities. They go toward shore excursions, bar tabs, ship stores, etc. Investors must own at least 100 shares to receive the credit. Present proof of ownership to the travel agent or cruise line to receive the credit.

Royal Caribbean also gives its shareholders that own a minimum of 100 shares at time of sailing on any Royal Caribbean®, Celebrity Cruises® or Azamara Club Cruises®, a nice little bonus. Shareholders receive:

- $250 Onboard Credit per Stateroom on Sailings of 14 or more nights.
- $200 Onboard Credit per Stateroom on Sailings of 10 to 13 nights.
- $100 Onboard Credit per Stateroom on Sailings of 6 to 9 nights.
- $50 Onboard Credit per Stateroom on Sailings of 5 nights or less.

In general, you will need to mail or fax either a shareholder proxy card or a copy or your brokerage statement to the company.

Spending traps on the cruise

Cruise ships have numerous ways to get you to part with your travel dollars when travelling.

Casino

Most cruise ships have a casino on board where you can gamble when you are at sea (not at port). This is a heavy temptation due to the location on board, usually located mid-ship.

Spa

Part of the problem with being on a cruise is the lack of competition for services. Featuring services from massages to thermal suite, Cruise line spas charge rates equal to high-end salons.

If you are looking for a spa day, try to take advantage of spa discounts typically offered on embarkation and port days. Check your ship's daily program for spa treatment specials that may be available one day only, or during certain hours.

On a cruise I took in December of 2012, for a day in port, I saw a special for $42 instead of $97 for a haircut, shampoo, and colour.

Alcohol

Alcoholic beverages and wine are not included in your cruise price. Drinking on a cruise is not inexpensive, but the prices you will pay are similar to a restaurant.

Most cruise ships advertise discounted **daily drink specials** you may want to try on some ships.

Look for events on the cruise that offer free drinks, such as the art auctions, or at the Captain's cocktail parties.

A great promotion I saw recently was a wine maker's class on board the MSC Poesia. This class provided three bottles of wine for a cost of $40.

Check with your cruise ship prior to embarkation for their policy on bringing wine. They may allow wine with the payment of a corkage fee.

Soft drinks

Most cruise lines will charge a flat access fee for unlimited pop for the whole week for children and adult passengers. A sample price for the last 10-day cruise I took was $49 USD.

One thing to remember is that you are allowed to bring your own soft drinks.

Just save a little room when packing because you can pack a few 2L plastic bottles of your favourite soft drink to bring for the cruise.

Photos

All cruise ship lines love to capture those special moments with your family. Photographers are ready at embarkation, and at most gala nights on board. The photographers are professional and know how to turn everyone into a glamorous movie star.

The photographers have quality lighting to work with, and incredible sets, but remember that an 8 x 10 print can cost as much as $20 on most cruise ships.

My recommendation is to take many photos with your digital camera, as most will be high enough quality to make an 8 x 10 photo.

Do not feel pressured to have your photo taken, or feel the requirement to purchase the photos. Even if you don't buy any photos, I always have fun checking them out in the gallery.

Internet Access

As connected as I am, I tend to stay off of my PC when travelling to have a break from technology.

If you are determined to check your email, avoid the cruise ship's costly charges. On the last cruise I took, the ship charged $24 for 60 minutes of access.

Remember that the Internet access is not always guaranteed, and you may experience interruptions.

Some Internet services, websites and applications such as VPN, remote connection may be restricted for company Policy.

When you need to check your email, bring a netbook or a tablet, and you should be able to find many restaurants or shops that have free WIFI (Starbucks or McDonalds) or WIFI with a purchase near the port. I tend to find the shops that do not have free WIFI have a faster connection, because fewer people are using the connection.

Discounted sailing for children

Some cruise lines allow kids to sail for a discounted cost or free (you just need to pay the port taxes).

MSC Cruises

Children 11 and younger sail free and children 12-17 sail at a reduced rate on every MSC Cruises sailing. Children 11 and under sail free when sailing as 3rd / 4th guests in the same stateroom as two full-fare paying guests.

MSC Cruises even has a kids' club where they have organized activities for children of different ages.

Norwegian Cruise Lines*

They offer significantly discounted rates for the 3rd - 8th guests. Infants under six months of age are not eligible for travel on Norwegian ships.

Disney Cruise Line

Children do not sail for free; however, since they will be travelling with two paying adults, they would pay a discounted rate. During the low season, Disney has special offers where children under 17 sail for free (they will still need to pay port fees and taxes).

Royal Caribbean*

They do not have a discount, however, if you book a stateroom with two paying adults, a third person can occupy the room as well for a discounted rate. Infants must be at least six months old to sail with Royal Caribbean, but for any transatlantic cruises or cruises that requires more than three days at sea, children must be 12 months old on the date of departure.

Carnival Cruises*

Carnival® charges full price for infants and children, but gratuities do not apply to guests less than two years of age.

Understand Cabin differences

As a four-time cruiser, I have stayed in many different ships, and experienced a variety of cabins. The more expensive cabins and the outside cabin are more enjoyable experiences if you plan to spend an extended period of time in your cabin (i.e. small child napping). The only major benefit is a small lounge area that has a small coffee table and sofa).

Look at the price differences between the two cabins and evaluate if the extra room is worth it.

Understand all the fees

Look carefully for information on service fees, government taxes and port charges, which often aren't included in the sale price.

Tools

- Cruise Compete - http://www.cruisecompete.com

- Compass Speakers - http://www.compassspeakers.com

- Sixth Star - http://www.sixthstar.com

- Carnival Cruises Shareholder Bonus – http://www.canadiantravelhacking.com/go/carnival-bonus

- Royal Caribbean Shareholder Bonus – http://www.canadiantravelhacking.com/go/rccl-bonus

- Viator - http://www.viator.com

Appendices

Appendix 1: Interview with a Flight Centre Manager

I had the fortune of being able to interview Aaron Levine, a Manager from a Flight Centre in Toronto, Ontario.

He gave me some valuable tips and advice on now just what added benefits a travel consultant can do but what to look for when booking with a travel consultant.

1. **What exactly does a Flight Centre travel consultant do for a client (what is the booking process when I come into a retail store)?**

    After a client is greeted, we ask a lot of questions to find out not only where a client wants to go but more-so what the client is looking to experience and their expectations. Due to the multitude of travel options, every inquiry is a little different each coming with their own solutions based upon the amount of time they have to travel and their budget.

    The key difference between booking with a Flight Centre consultant and trying to do it yourself direct with a supplier or through an online agency, is our qualified advice and expertise. Our consultants will help you to make the best decisions for your travel requirements, based on your needs and wants in a fully holistic fashion, not just on price or timetables. There is much more to consider when planning a trip than the sticker price. We have teamed up with the leaders in every major travel segment to be able to offer our clients the best experience that suits their style and budget. We also have access to special fares and products that are simply not available elsewhere.

2. **With the number of Internet travel websites, why would a savvy traveler use a travel consultant from Flight Centre?**

We're here for you every step of the way (from booking the trip, any changes you need. In case the airline cancels the flight and also once you're in destination). We have access to special wholesale rates and advise our customers when adjusting a trip by a couple of hours or even a day before/after could save a large amount of money.

Our office/team has a meeting every morning to go over the latest industry news to give our customers the best travel advice and the most relevant information (The Internet won't decipher between the best airports to connect through based upon possible delays.) We are constantly attending trainings and workshops to ensure to ensure that we are offering the best and most up to date knowledge and travel advice. We offer expert advice as our office has a combined 70+ years of experience as travel consultants.

3. What is your favourite experience booking a travel experience for someone?

A client of mine was turning 60 and wanted to climb to Everest Base Camp (17,598 feet). She trained for over a year and while she kept me updated on her training, I kept her updated on what to expect during the hike. I sent her pictures for her upcoming trip for motivation.

She went on the trip and upon her return she went through every single picture with me and kept saying how this trip changed her life. It was an amazing moment and just another reason why I love what I do.

4. What are some benefits that travelers do not realize they receive when they booking with a seasoned travel agent?

Experience (the people in our office have been to most countries in the world - we share information so when you contact one person in our office you have a team of 8 people helping you). We can draw on support and specialized knowledge from any one of the other 1000+ consultants working for Flight Centre across Canada.

We get to know our customers preferences and ensure they are getting the maximum points on a flight:

- The best seats available

- The full details on baggage fees.

- The best amenities that the client really appreciates at their hotel/resorts and any possible upgrades.

5. **What are some questions to ask a travel consultant to see if they are qualified to handle a booking?**

I would ask a couple of simple questions:

1. What excites you about travel? Good travel consultants love to travel and they share that passion with their clients. They are there not only to guide you through the booking process and options, but also to help inspire and educate you

2. If you needed to make the trip I am contemplating, what would be important to you? A travel consultant may not have the same tastes as their clients, but they should know what would suit their client and be excited about helping to provide that experience.

6. **What are some ways where you saved time or money for your clients?**

We have access to special wholesale rates that can reduce the overall cost (i.e. last minute Toronto to Dallas booking within 7 days of departure can be over $1000 while our wholesale costs can cut this in 1/2 - based on space available.)

We can help with All Inclusive Package bookings. The Internet is a maze of different properties all with pristine pictures (usually empty) of every resort in the market. We have the experience from both booking and experiencing properties first hand to quickly match the right property to the right customer based upon budget and expectation.

Some great clients of mine were traveling in Greece and their son (17 years old) was leaving earlier than the rest of the family. He took a ferry from the island the family was staying on to Athens and on to the airport to make his flight home. When he got there the flight was canceled and no one was at the airline's desk. His mother called me (late in the day here in Toronto) and I stayed at the office until past midnight getting the client protected and re-ticketed with one of the airline's partners. This client's mother was so relieved and it felt great knowing that I was able to assist and relieve the stress for the family.

Made in the USA
Charleston, SC
29 April 2014